A practical foundation in accounting:
a student's solution guide

A practical foundation in accounting: a student's solution guide

HARRY JOHNSON and AUSTIN WHITTAM

Department of Accounting and Finance,
Manchester Polytechnic, Manchester

London
George Allen & Unwin
Boston   Sydney

George Allen & Unwin (Publishers) Ltd,
40 Museum Street, London WC1A 1LU, UK

George Allen & Unwin (Publishers) Ltd,
Park Lane, Hemel Hempstead, Herts HP2 4TE, UK

Allen & Unwin Inc.,
9 Winchester Terrace, Winchester, Mass 01890, USA

George Allen & Unwin Australia Pty Ltd,
8 Napier Street, North Sydney, NSW 2060, Australia

First published in 1982
Second impression 1983
Second edition 1984
Second impression 1984

British Library Cataloguing in Publication Data

Johnson, Harry, *1931–*
    A practical foundation in accountancy:
a student's solution guide.
1. Accounting—Problems, exercises, etc.
I. Title   II. Whittam, Austin
657′0.76   HF5661
ISBN 0–04–332096–1

Printed and bound in Great Britain by
Anchor Brendon Ltd, Tiptree, Essex

Contents

Contents

A note for students

As stated in the main text, the questions at the end of each chapter should be regarded as an integral part of that chapter. This student's guide gives suggested solutions to the 'S' suffixed questions. The same style and manner of presentation has been used in the solutions to the questions as is used in the examples in the main text.

Students should be aware of the fact that there are many different systems in practice, all of which achieve the same end of providing financial information. There are also different ways of setting out an answer to an accounting question, all of which would be considered correct.

Suggested method of working

Before attending a lecture

Read the appropriate chapter so that you will have some idea what the lecturer is explaining.

During the lecture

Make notes, particularly of any examples the lecturer shows.

After the lecture

Read the appropriate chapter again together with your lecture notes, making sure you understand all the examples. Do not attempt to learn by rote – it is a mistake!

Before attempting the homework required by your lecturer, work as many of the 'S' suffixed questions as time will allow. Do not consult the solution to a question until you have independently attempted a solution of your own. When you are satisfied that your solution is correct, or you understand where you have gone wrong, attempt the next question. The questions have been arranged in order of increasing difficulty to help your understanding, and to enable you to build on a firm foundation. When you have worked as many of the 'S' suffixed questions as time permits, attempt your homework problems. Remember that understanding *why* an answer you submitted was wrong is part of the learning process. If you do not understand why your solution is incorrect, ask your tutor.

1

Introduction to the double entry system of book-keeping

1.1S   (a) Assets – things owned
 (b) Liabilities – amounts owed
 (c) Capital – owner's or proprietor's interest

1.2S   The *accounting equation* is

$$\text{Capital} = \text{Assets} - \text{Liabilities}.$$

It means that the amount invested in the business by the proprietor is equal to the things owned by the business less the amounts owed by the business.

1.3S

	Assets	Liabilities	Capital
(a) Buildings	√		
(b) Loan to the firm		√	
(c) Equipment	√		
(d) Cash	√		
(e) Cash paid into the firm's bank account by the proprietor	√		√

2 Ledger accounts or 'T' accounts

2.1S

	Debit	*Credit*
(a)	Bank	Capital
(b)	Shop premises	Bank
(c)	Fixtures and fittings	Bank
(d)	Bank	C. Gull – loan
(e)	Motor van	Bank
(f)	Office equipment	Bank

2.2S

Bank

19X1		£	19X1		£
Jan.	1 Capital	50,000	Jan.	3 Shop premises	21,000
	17 C. Gull – loan	5,000		10 Fixtures and fittings	3,000
				24 Motor van	3,500
				31 Office equipment	250
				31 Balance c/d	27,250
		55,000			55,000
Feb.	1 Balance b/d	27,250			

Capital

			19X1		£
			Jan.	1 Bank	50,000

Fixtures and fittings

19X1	£		
Jan. 10 Bank	3,000		

Motor van

19X1	£		
Jan. 24 Bank	3,500		

Shop premises

19X1	£		
Jan. 3 Bank	21,000		

C. Gull – loan

		19X1	£
		Jan. 17 Bank	5,000

Office equipment

19X1	£		
Jan. 31 Bank	250		

Trial Balance — A. Sparrow

	Dr. £	Cr. £
Bank	27,250	
Capital		50,000
Shop premises	21,000	
Fixtures and fittings	3,000	
C. Gull – loan		5,000
Motor van	3,500	
Office equipment	250	
	55,000	55,000

Balance Sheet as at 31 January 19X1

	£
Assets	
Shop premises	21,000
Motor van	3,500
Fixtures and fittings	3,000
Office equipment	250
Bank	27,250
	55,000
Financed by	
Capital	50,000
C. Gull – loan	5,000
	55,000

3 Trading

3.1S

The ledger of D. Johnstone

Bank

19X1		£	19X1		£
Jan.	2 Capital	50,000	Jan.	3 Shop premises	20,000
	19 Sales	8,500		5 Shopfittings	2,500
	31 J. Parker	2,000		9 Purchases	14,000
				10 Cash	100
				16 Van	2,500
				23 Van expenses	15
				31 Balance c/d	21,385
		60,500			60,500
Feb.	1 Balance b/d	21,385			

Capital

			19X1		£
			Jan.	2 Bank	50,000

Shop premises

19X1		£		
Jan.	3 Bank	20,000		

Shopfittings

19X1		£		
Jan.	5 Bank	2,5000		

Purchases

19X1		£		£
Jan.	9 Bank	14,000	(Trading account	14,000)

6

Cash

19X1	£	19X1	£
Jan. 10 Bank	100	Jan. 12 Stationery	20
		28 Cleaning	20
		31 Balance c/d	60
	100		100
Feb. 1 Balance b/d	60		

Stationery

19X1	£		£
Jan. 12 Cash	20	(Profit and loss a/c	20)

Van

19X1	£		
Jan. 16 Bank	2,500		

Sales

19X1	£	19X1	£
Jan. 31 Balance c/d	12,000	Jan. 19 Bank	8,500
		Jan. 26 J. Parker	3,500
	12,000		12,000
(Trading a/c	12,000)	Feb. 1 Balance b/d	12,000

Van expenses

19X1	£		£
Jan. 21 Bank	15	(Profit and loss a/c	15)

J. Parker

19X1	£	19X1	£
Jan. 26 Sales	3,500	Jan. 31 Bank	2,000
		31 Balance c/d	1,500
	3,500		3,500
Feb. 1 Balance b/d	1,500		

Cleaning

19X1	£		£
Jan. 28 Cash	20	(Profit and loss a/c	20)

D. Johnstone
Extended trial balance

	Trial balance		Trading account		Profit and loss account		Balance sheet	
	Dr. £	*Cr.* £	*Dr.* £	*Cr.* £	*Dr.* £	*Cr.* £	*Dr.* £	*Cr.* £
Bank	21,385						21,385	
Capital		50,000						50,000
Shop premises	20,000						20,000	
Shopfittings	2,500						2,500	
Purchases	14,000		14,000					
Cash	60						60	
Stationery	20				20			
Van	2,500						2,500	
Sales		12,000		12,000				
Van expenses	15				15			
J. Parker (debtor)	1,500						1,500	
Cleaning	20				20			
Closing stock		4,000		4,000				
Closing stock c/f	4,000						4,000	
GROSS PROFIT			2,000			2,000		
NET PROFIT					1,945			1,945
	66,000	66,000	16,000	16,000	2,000	2,000	51,945	51,945

D. Johnstone
Trading and Profit and Loss Account
for the month ended 31 January 19X1

	£	£
Sales		12,000
Cost of sales		
Purchases	14,000	
less Closing stock	4,000	10,000
Gross profit		2,000
Stationery	20	
Van expenses	15	
Cleaning	20	55
Net profit		1,945

Balance Sheet as at 31 January 19X1

	£	£
Assets		
Fixed assets		
Shop premises		20,000
Shopfittings		2,500
Van		2,500
		25,000
Current assets		
Stock	4,000	
Debtor	1,500	
Bank	21,385	
Cash	60	26,945
		51,945
Financed by		
Capital		50,000
add Profit for the month		1,945
		51,945

3.2S

The ledger of P. Brown
Bank

19X2		£	19X2		£
Jul. 1	Capital	20,000	Jul. 1	Shopfittings	2,000
31	Cash	1,375	1	Van	3,200
			2	Rent	200
			10	Insurance	12
			17	J. Smith	1,500
			27	I. Thomas	700
			31	Balance c/d	13,763
		21,375			21,375
Aug. 1	Balance b/d	13,763			

Capital

				19X2		£
				Jul. 1 Bank		20,000

Shopfittings

19X2		£		
Jul. 1 Bank		2,000		

Van

19X2		£		
Jul. 1 Bank		3,200		

Rent

19X2		£			£
Jul. 2 Bank		200		(Profit and loss a/c	200)

Purchases

19X2		£	19X2		£
Jul. 3 J. Smith		2,500	Jul. 15 J. Smith		480
19 I. Thomas		1,400	31 Balance c/d		3,420
		3,900			3,900
Aug. 1 Balance b/d		3,420	(Trading a/c		3,420)

J. Smith

19X2		£	19X2		£
Jul. 15 Purchases		480	Jul. 3 Purchases		2,500
17 Bank		1,500			
31 Balance c/d		520			
		2,500			2,500
			Aug. 1 Balance b/d		520

Cash

19X2		£	19X2		£
Jul. 5	Sales	260	Jul. 8	Wages	35
12	Sales	400	15	Wages	35
19	Sales	480	22	Wages	35
26	Sales	600	24	Stationery	25
			29	Wages	35
			31	Bank	1,375
			31	Balance c/d	200
		1,740			1,740
Aug. 1	Balance b/d	200			

Sales

19X2		£	19X2		£
Jul. 31	Balance c/d	1,740	Jul. 5	Cash	260
			12	Cash	400
			19	Cash	480
			26	Cash	600
		1,740			1,740
	(Trading a/c	1,740)	Aug. 1	Balance b/d	1,740

Wages

19X2		£	19X2		£
Jul. 8	Cash	35	Jul. 31	Balance c/d	140
15	Cash	35			
22	Cash	35			
29	Cash	35			
		140			140
Aug. 1	Balance b/d	140		(Profit and loss a/c	140)

Insurance

19X2		£			£
Jul. 10	Bank	12		(Profit and loss a/c	12)

I. Thomas

19X2		£	19X2		£
Jul. 27	Bank	700	Jul. 19	Purchases	1,400
31	Balance c/d	700			
		1,400			1,400
			Aug. 1	Balance b/d	700

Stationery

19X2		£			£
Jul. 24	Cash	25		(Profit and loss a/c	25)

P. Brown
Extended trial balance

	Trial balance Dr. £	Trial balance Cr. £	Trading account Dr. £	Trading account Cr. £	Profit and loss account Dr. £	Profit and loss account Cr. £	Balance sheet Dr. £	Balance sheet Cr. £
Bank	13,763						13,763	
Capital		20,000						20,000
Shopfittings	2,000						2,000	
Van	3,200						3,200	
Rent	200				200			
Purchases	3,420		3,420					
J. Smith (creditor)		520						520
Cash	200						200	
Sales		1,740		1,740				
Wages	140				140			
Insurance	12				12			
I. Thomas (creditor)		700						700
Stationery	25				25			
Closing stock		2,715		2,715				
Closing stock c/f	2,715						2,715	
GROSS PROFIT			1,035			1,035		
NET PROFIT					658			658
	25,675	25,675	4,455	4,455	1,035	1,035	21,878	21,878

P. Brown
Trading and Profit and Loss Account
for the month ended 31 July 19X2

	£	£
Sales		1,740
Cost of sales		
Purchases	3,420	
less Closing stock	2,715	705
Gross profit		1,035
Rent	200	
Wages	140	
Insurance	12	
Stationery	25	377
		658

Balance Sheet as at 31 July 19X2

	£	£
Assets		
Fixed assets		
Shopfittings		2,000
Van		3,200
		5,200
Current assets		
Stock	2,715	
Bank	13,763	
Cash	200	
	16,678	
less Current liabilities		
Creditors	1,220	15,458
		20,658
Financed by		
Capital		20,000
add Profit for the month		658
		20,658

4 Final accounts

4.1S

John Pink's ledger
Rent account

19X5	£	19X5	£
Mar. 30 Bank	100	Dec. 31 Profit and loss	400
Jun. 28 Bank	100		
Sep. 30 Bank	100		
Dec. 31 Amount owing c/d	100		
	400		400
		19X6	
		Jan. 1 Amount owing b/d	100

4.2S

Charles Indigo's ledger
Rent account

19X6	£	19X7	£
Sep. 28 Bank	250	Jun. 30 Profit and loss	1,000
19X7			
Jan. 3 Bank	250		
Mar. 28 Bank	250		
Jun. 30 Amount owing c/d	250		
	1,000		1,000
		Jul. 1 Amount owing b/d	250

Rates account

19X6	£	19X7	£
Jul. 28 Bank	220	Jun. 30 Prepayment c/d	140
19X7		30 Profit and loss	360
Apr. 30 Bank	280		
	500		500
Jul. 1 Prepayment b/d	140		

14

J. Black
Trading and Profit and Loss Account
for the year ended 31 December 19X8

	£	£	£
Sales			63,000
Cost of sales			
Stock at 1 January 19X8		10,800	
Purchases	53,500		
less Purchase returns	2,000	51,500	
		62,300	
less Stock at 31 December			
19X8		11,900	50,400
Gross profit			12,600
less Expenses			
Rent and rates		2,520	
Lighting and heating		470	
General expenses		1,000	3,990
Net profit			8,610

Note
Lighting and heating

	£
Per trial balance	440
add Amount accrued	30
	470

Balance Sheet as at 31 December 19X8

	£	£	£
Assets			
Fixed assets			
Fixtures and fittings			12,800
Motor vehicles			7,500
			20,300
Current assets			
Stock		11,900	
Debtors		4,450	
Cash in hand		80	
		16,430	
less Current liabilities			
Creditors and accrual	2,900		
Bank overdraft	4,780	7,680	
Working capital			8,750
			29,050

Financed by
Capital

	£
Balance at 1 January 19X8	30,000
add Profit for the year	8,610
	38,610
less Drawings	9,560
	29,050

Note

Creditors and accrual

	£
Creditors per trial balance	2,870
add Electricity accrued	30
	2,900

4.4S

S. White
Trading and Profit and Loss Account
for the year ended 30 June 19X6

	£	£	£
Sales			24,708
less Sales returns			180
			24,528
Cost of sales			
Stock at 1 July 19X5		7,296	
Purchases	17,434		
less Purchase returns	199	17,235	
		24,531	
less Stock at 30 June 19X6		7,144	17,387
Gross profit			7,141
add Discounts received			186
			7,327
less Expenses			
Salaries		1,245	
Rates		300	
Lighting and heating		200	
Sundry expenses		162	
Discounts allowed		330	2,237
Net profit			5,090

Notes
1. Rates

	£
Per trial balance	400
less Paid in advance	100
	300

2. Lighting and heating

	£
Per trial balance	172
add Amount accrued	28
	200

Balance Sheet as at 30 June 19X6

	£	£
Assets		
Fixed assets		
Freehold premises		15,000
Fixtures and fittings		6,750
		21,750
Current assets		
Stock	7,144	
Debtors and prepayment	3,280	
Cash at bank	2,908	
Cash in hand	30	
	13,362	
less Current liabilities		
Creditors and accrual	2,272	
Working capital		11,090
		32,840
Financed by		
Capital		
Balance at 1 July 19X5		30,000
add Profit for the year		5,090
		35,090
less Drawings		2,250
		32,840

17

Notes

1. Debtors and prepayments

	£
Debtors per trial balance	3,180
add Rates paid in advance	100
	3,280

2. Creditors and accruals

	£
Creditors per trial balance	2,244
add Electricity accrued	28
	2,272

4.5S

B. Riley's ledger
Rent and rates

19X3		£	19X3		£
Jan. 1	Rates prepaid b/d	88	Jan. 1	Rent outstanding b/d	190
4	Bank – rent	190	Dec. 31	Profit and loss	1,124
Mar. 29	Bank – rent	190			
Jun. 26	Bank – rates	184			
Jul. 7	Bank – rent	190			
Sep. 30	Bank – rent	190			
Dec. 28	Bank – rent	190			
Dec. 31	Rates owing c/d	92			
		1,314			1,314
			19X4		
			Jan. 1	Rates owing b/d	92

Check of total charged to profit and loss account:

	£
Rent for the year (4 × £190)	760
Rates: for 3 months to 31 March 19X3	88
for 6 months to 30 September 19X3	184
for 3 months to 31 December 19X3	92
	1,124

5 Depreciation

5.1S

Truck & Co.
Plant and machinery

19X7		£	19X8		£
Oct. 1 Balance b/d		10,000	Sep. 30 Balance c/d		10,000
19X8					
Oct. 1 Balance b/d		10,000			

Provision for depreciation of plant and machinery

19X8		£	19X7		£
Sep. 30 Balance c/d		4,000	Oct. 1 Balance b/d		2,000
			19X8		
			Sep. 30 Profit and loss		2,000
		4,000			4,000
			Oct. 1 Balance b/d		4,000

Balance Sheet (extract) as at 30 September 19X8

	Cost	Depreciation	Net
Fixed assets			
	£	£	£
Plant and machinery	10,000	4,000	6,000

5.2S

D. Bird
Machinery

19X2		£	19X2		£
Jun. 30 Bank		3,000	Dec. 31 Balance c/d		3,000
19X3			19X3		
Jan. 1 Balance b/d		3,000	Dec. 31 Balance c/d		3,000
19X4			19X4		
Jan. 1 Balance b/d		3,000	Dec. 31 Balance c/d		3,000

19X5				19X5		
Jan. 1	Balance b/d	3,000		Dec. 31	Balance c/d	3,000
19X6				19X6		
Jan. 1	Balance b/d	3,000		Dec. 31	Balance c/d	3,000
19X7				19X7		
Jan. 1	Balance b/d	3,000		Dec. 31	Balance c/d	3,000
19X8						
Jan. 1	Balance b/d	3,000				

Provision for depreciation of machinery

		£				£
19X2				19X2		
Dec. 31	Balance c/d	750		Dec. 31	Profit and loss	750
19X3				19X3		
Dec. 31	Balance c/d	1,312		Jan. 1	Balance b/d	750
				Dec. 31	Profit and loss	562
		1,312				1,312
19X4				19X4		
Dec. 31	Balance c/d	1,734		Jan. 1	Balance b/d	1,312
				Dec. 31	Profit and loss	422
		1,734				1,734
19X5				19X5		
Dec. 31	Balance c/d	2,051		Jan. 1	Balance b/d	1,734
				Dec. 31	Profit and loss	317
		2,051				2,051
19X6				19X6		
Dec. 31	Balance c/d	2,288		Jan. 1	Balance b/d	2,051
				Dec. 31	Profit and loss	237
		2,288				2,288
19X7				19X7		
Dec. 31	Balance c/d	2,466		Jan. 1	Balance b/d	2,288
				Dec. 31	Profit and loss	178
		2,466				2,466
				19X8		
				Jan. 1	Balance b/d	2,466

Tutorial notes

1. Applying the formula given in the text, the rate per cent is found to be

$$1 - \sqrt[6]{\frac{534}{3,000}} = 1 - 0.75 = 25\%.$$

2. Since the depreciation is to be calculated on the reducing value of the asset, the charge to profit and loss will obviously reduce each year, viz.

		£
Year 1	Cost	3,000
	Depreciation 25% × £3,000	750
Year 2	Book value	2,250
	Depreciation 25% × £2,250	562
Year 3	Book value	1,688

and so on

5.3S (a)

Machine tools

19X4		£	19X4		£
Jan. 1 Balance b/d		10,000	Jan. 1 Disposal of machine tools		5,000
Jan. 1 Bank		8,000	Dec. 31 Balance c/d		13,000
		18,000			18,000
19X5					
Jan. 1 Balance b/d		13,000			

Office machinery

19X4		£	19X4		£
Jan. 1 Balance b/d		2,000	Dec. 31 Balance c/d		2,000
19X5					
Jan. 1 Balance b/d		2,000			

Provision for depreciation of machine tools

19X4		£	19X4		£
Jan. 1	Disposal of machine tools	1,000	Jan. 1	Balance b/d	2,000
Dec. 31	Balance c/d	3,400	Dec. 31	Profit and loss	2,400
		4,400			4,400
			19X5		
			Jan. 1	Balance b/d	3,400

Provision for depreciation of office machinery

19X4		£	19X4		£
Dec. 31	Balance c/d	600	Jan. 1	Balance b/d	300
			Dec. 31	Profit and loss	300
		600			600
			19X5		
			Jan. 1	Balance b/d	600

Disposal of machine tools

19X4		£	19X4		£
Jan. 1	Machine tools	5,000	Jan. 1	Provision for depreciation of machine tools	1,000
			Jan. 1	Bank	2,750
			Dec. 31	Profit and loss	1,250
		5,000			5,000

(b) Depreciation may be defined as the apportionment of the cost of an asset, less any residual value, over its working life on a consistent, defined basis. It does not of itself provide any cash for replacement. A separate transaction transferring the cash from the bank to a special fund would be necessary. In any case, since the depreciation charge in conventional accounts is based upon the historic cost of the asset, such a transfer of cash, if based upon the depreciation charge, will not provide sufficient funds to replace an asset in times of inflation.

Tutorial note

The charge to profit and loss of £2,400 for the year to 31 December 19X4 shown in the provision for depreciation of machine tools account is calculated as 20% on £12,000 = £2,400, i.e.

£4,000 the written down value of the machine purchased on 1 January 19X3, and still held at 31 December 19X4, plus

£8,000 the cost of the machine tool acquired on 1 January 19X4

£12,000

5.4S (a)   Motor vehicles

19X6		£	19X6		£
May 31	Bank – NOL862V	18,000	Dec. 31	Balance c/d	42,000
Oct. 31	Bank – NOM760W	24,000			
		42,000			42,000
19X7			19X7		
Jan. 1	Balance b/d	42,000	Sep. 1	Motor vehicle disposals	18,000
			Dec. 31	Balance c/d	24,000
		42,000			42,000
19X8					
Jan. 1	Balance b/d	24,000			

(b)   Provision for depreciation of motor vehicles

19X6		£	19X6		£
Dec. 31	Balance c/d	2,900	Dec. 31	Profit and loss	2,900
19X7			19X7		
Sep. 1	Motor vehicles disposals	4,500	Jan. 1	Balance b/d	2,900
Dec. 31	Balance c/d	5,600	Dec. 31	Profit and loss	7,200
		10,100			10,100
			19X8		
			Jan. 1	Balance b/d	5,600

(c)   Motor vehicles disposals

19X7		£	19X7		£
Sep. 1	Motor vehicles	18,000	Sep. 1	Provision for depreciation of motor vehicles	4,500
			Sep. 20	Bank – insurance proceeds	12,500
			Dec. 31	Profit and loss	1,000
		18,000			18,000

Tutorial notes:

1. The depreciation charge is calculated as follows:

Vehicle No.	Cost £		19X6 £		19X7 £
NOL 862V	18,000	7 months at 20% p.a.	2,100	8 months at 20% p.a.	2,400
NOM 760W	24,000	2 months at 20% p.a.	800	12 months at 20% p.a.	4,800
			2,900		7,200

2. Since the first vehicle purchased, NOL 862V, is no longer held by the firm, the balance on the motor vehicles account at 31 December 19X7 should be the cost of the second vehicle purchased, NOM 760W, and the balance on the provision for depreciation of motor vehicles account at the same date should be the depreciation provided to that date on that vehicle. An examination of the two accounts will confirm their correctness.

5.5S

F. Robinson
Trading and Profit and Loss Account
for the year ended 30 June 19X9

	£	£	£
Sales			164,720
less Returns inwards			1,330
			163,390
Cost of sales			
Stock at 1 July 19X8		14,864	
Purchases	116,230		
less Returns outwards	1,910	114,320	
		129,184	
less Stock at 30 June 19X9		10,280	118,904
Gross profit			44,486
add Discount receivable			816
			45,302
less Expenses			
Salaries and commission		18,600	
Rent, rates and insurance		2,050	
Lighting and heating		1,510	
Sundry expenses		802	
Discount allowed		1,220	
Depreciation of fixtures and fittings		400	24,582
Net profit			20,720

Notes

1. Salaries and commission

	£
Per trial balance	18,360
add Commission owing	240
Profit and loss a/c	18,600

2. Rent, rates and insurance

	£	£
Per trial balance		2,600
add Rent owing		250
		2,850
less Rates prepaid	700	
Insurance prepaid	100	800
Profit and loss a/c		2,050

3. Depreciation of fixtures and fittings 10% per annum on £4,000 = £400.

Balance Sheet as at 30 June 19X9

Assets

Fixed assets	Cost £	Depreciation £	Net £
Freehold premises	16,000		16,000
Fixtures and fittings	4,000	2,000	2,000
	20,000	2,000	18,000

Current assets		
Stock	10,280	
Debtors and prepayments	13,010	
Cash at bank	2,164	
Cash in hand	50	
	25,504	
less Current liabilities		
Creditors	12,184	
Working capital		13,320
		31,320

Financed by		
Capital		
Balance at 1 July 19X8		21,800
add Profit for the year		20,720
		42,520
less Drawings		11,200
		31,320

Notes
1. The figure of £2,000 shown as depreciation of fixtures and fittings is the accumulated amount to date, i.e. £1,600 to 30 June 19X8 plus £400 for the year to 30 June 19X9.
2. Debtors and prepayments

	£
Per trial balance	12,210
add Rates prepaid	700
Insurance prepaid	100
	13,010

3. Creditors

	£
Per trial balance	11,694
add Rent owing	250
Commission owing	240
	12,184

5.6S

S. Barnard
Trading and Profit and Loss Account
for the year ended 31 December 19X8

	£	£	£
Sales			38,700
less Sales returns			1,650
			37,050
Cost of sales			
Stock at 1 January 19X8		8,200	
Purchases	26,100		
less Purchase returns	1,300	24,800	
		33,000	
less Stock at 31 December 19X8		11,500	21,500
Gross profit			15,550
add Discount received			1,150
			16,700
less Expenses			
Wages		2,450	
Rent and rates		2,000	
Insurance		840	
Depreciation of – Van	550		
– Fixtures and fittings	250	800	6,090
Net profit			10,610

Notes

1. Rent and rates

	£
Per trial balance	2,110
add Rent owing	250
	2,360
less Rates prepaid	360
Profit and loss	2,000

2. Insurance

	£
Per trial balance	1,030
less Insurance prepaid	190
Profit and loss	840

3. Depreciation: The annual depreciation charge on the van is £(2,500 − 300) ÷ 4 = £550. The annual depreciation charge on the fixtures and fittings is £(2,590 − 90) ÷ 10 = £250.

Balance Sheet as at 31 December 19X8

Assets

	Cost £	Depreciation £	Net £
Fixed assets			
Fixtures and fittings	2,590	1,500	1,090
Van	2,500	1,650	850
	5,090	3,150	1,940
Current assets			
Stock		11,500	
Debtors and prepayments		3,080	
Cash at bank		8,750	
Cash in hand		30	
		23,360	
less Current liabilities			
Creditors		3,000	20,360
			22,300
Financed by			
Capital			
Balance at 1 January 19X8			18,000
add Profit for the year			10,610
			28,610
less Drawings			6,310
			22,300

Notes

1. The depreciation to date is calculated as follows:

	Furniture and fittings £	Van £
Accumulated to 1 January 19X8	1,250	1,100
add Charge for the year	250	550
Balance sheet	1,500	1,650

2. Debtors and prepayments

	£
Per trial balance	2,530
add Rates prepaid	360
Insurance prepaid	190
	3,080

3. Creditors

	£
Per trial balance	2,750
add Rent owing	250
	3,000

6 Division of the ledger: books of original entry

6.1S

J. Mowbray
Cash book

19X2		Cash £	Bank £	19X2		Cash £	Bank £
Jan. 1	Balances b/d	33	625	Jan. 4	J. Greaney		80
3	V. Banyard	107		5	Bank	40	
4	I. Watson	20		6	Wages	100	
5	Cash		40	11	K. Walton		42
12	W. Larkin		75	13	Cash		90
13	Bank	90			Wages	100	
15	A. Benthram		150	19	Office Equip-ment Co.	8	
18	J. Noble		86	20	Wages	100	
20	J. Jones	106		24	A.Williamson		55
25	P. Willey		152	27	Cash		110
27	Bank	110			Wages	100	
				31	Balances c/d	18	751
		466	1,128			466	1,128
Feb. 1	Balances b/d	18	751				

6.2S (a)

A. M. Smith
Cash book

19X3		Discount £	Cash £	Bank £	19X3		Discount £	Cash £	Bank £
Jan. 1	Balance b/d			520	Jan. 1	Cash			180
	Bank		180		3	Postages		15	
2	N. Walton	26		494	8	R. Hayton	18		342
10	W. Bolton			653	11	H. Vanstone			300
14	Bank		135			Wages		120	
21	D. Webster	21		399	14	Cash			135
28	Bank		174		16	C. Yates	6		114
					25	Wages		120	
						Stationery		28	
						Postages		26	

29

	Dis-count £	Cash £	Bank £			Dis-count £	Cash £	Bank £
				28	Cash			174
					Drawings			280
				30	F. Wilson			153
				31	Balances c/d		180	388
	47	489	2,066			24	489	2,066
Feb. 1 Balances b/d		180	388					

(b) Discount allowed of £47 would be posted to the debit of the discount allowed account. Discount received of £24 would be posted to the credit of discount received account.

6.3S

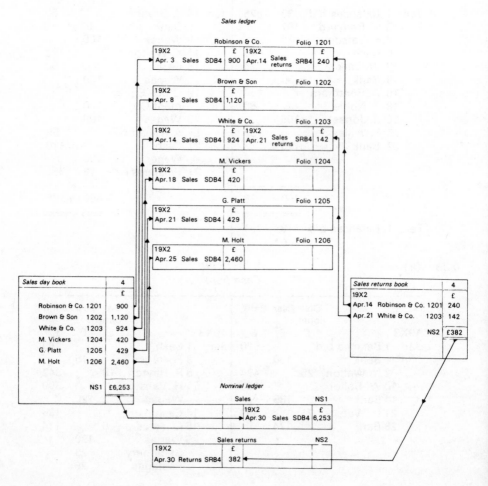

E. Booth
Sales Day Book   Folio 10

19X8			Folio	£
Oct.	1	M. Greenwood	DG2	1,240
	4	A Gaston	DG1	746
	6	E. Aldcroft	DA1	640
	10	M. Daniels	DD1	480
	14	M. Greenwood	DG2	420
	16	A. Gaston	DG1	264
	18	W. Pickles	DP1	336
	24	E. Aldcroft	DA1	348
		M. Daniels	DD1	260
	27	M. Heslop	DH1	760
	30	A. Crompton	DC1	920
	31	A. Gaston	DG1	647
			NS1	7,061

Purchases Day Book   Folio 10

19X8			Folio	£
Oct.	3	A. Hargreaves	CH1	800
	4	R. Scruton	CS1	420
	6	H. Smith	CS2	708
	18	A. Hargreaves	CH1	680
	21	B. Hubbard	CH2	2,240
	27	P. Davies	CD1	520
	30	E. Hull	CH3	1,460
			NP1	6,828

Debtors Ledger
E. Aldcroft   DA1

19X8				£	19X8		£
Oct.	6	Sales	SDB10	640	Oct. 31 Balance c/d		988
	24	Sales	SDB10	348			
				988			988
Nov.	1	Balance b/d		988			

A Crompton   DC1

19X8			£	19X8	£
Oct. 30 Sales		SDB10	920		

31

M. Daniels DD1

19X8		£	19X8	£
Oct. 10 Sales	SDB10	480	Oct. 31 Balance c/d	740
24 Sales	SDB10	260		
		740		740
Nov. 1 Balance b/d		740		

A. Gaston DG1

19X8		£	19X8	£
Oct. 4 Sales	SDB10	746	Oct. 31 Balance c/d	1,657
16 Sales	SDB10	264		
31 Sales	SDB10	647		
		1,657		1,657
Nov. 1 Balance b/d		1,657		

M. Greenwood DG2

19X8		£	19X8	£
Oct. 1 Sales	SDB10	1,240	Oct. 31 Balance c/d	1,660
14 Sales	SDB10	420		
		1,660		1,660
Nov. 1 Balance b/d		1,660		

M. Heslop DH1

19X8		£		
Oct. 27 Sales	SDB10	760		

W. Pickles DP1

19X8		£		
Oct. 18 Sales	SDB10	336		

Creditors Ledger
P. Davies CD1

			19X8	£
			Oct. 27 Purchases PDB10	520

A. Hargreaves CH1

19X8	£	19X8		£
Oct. 31 Balance c/d	1,480	Oct. 3 Purchases	PDB10	800
		18 Purchases	PDB10	680
	1,480			1,480
		Nov. 1 Balance b/d		1,480

B. Hubbard — CH2

			19X8			£
			Oct. 21 Purchases	PDB10		2,240

E. Hull — CH3

			19X8			£
			Oct. 30 Purchases	PDB10		1,460

R. Scruton — CS1

			19X8			£
			Oct. 4 Purchases	PDB10		420

H. Smith — CS2

			19X8			£
			Oct. 6 Purchases	PDB10		708

Nominal Ledger
Purchases — NP1

19X8			£			
Oct. 31 Purchases PDB10			6,828			

Sales — NS1

			19X8			£
			Oct. 31 Sales	SDB10		7,061

6.5S

J. Shaw
Journal

19X8		Dr. £	Cr. £
Jan. 1	Freehold premises	25,000	
	Fittings	12,000	
	Stock	8,000	
	E. Booth	480	
	M. Greenough	360	
	Cash	200	
	Loan – J. Buckle		10,000
	Bank		6,800
	A. Hargreaves		260
	Provision for depreciation of fittings		3,000
	Capital		25,980
		46,040	46,040

Assets and liabilities at
1 January 19X8.

33

J. Shaw
Journal

Folio 8/1

19X8			Dr.	Cr.
			£	£
Jan. 1	Freehold premises	F1	25,000	
	Fittings	F2	12,000	
	Stock	S1	8,000	
	E. Booth	B1	480	
	M. Greenough	G1	360	
	Cash	CB8/1	200	
	Loan – J. Buckle	B2		10,000
	Bank	CB8/1		6,800
	A. Hargreaves	H1		260
	Provision for deprecia-			
	tion on fittings	F2		3,000
	Capital	C1		25,980
			46,040	46,040

Assets and liabilities at
1 January 19X8.

Note

The journal entry to record the opening balances as required by
Question 6.5S has been repeated above for illustration purposes.

Journal (cont.)

			Dr.	Cr.
Jan. 18	Fittings	F2	1,200	
	N. Barrow	B3		1,200
	Purchase of fittings –			
	see invoice no. 1234			
	dated 18 January 19X8.			

Sales Day Book

Folio 8/1

19X8		Folio	£
Jan. 2	E. Booth	B1	290
5	M. Greenough	G1	360
14	C. Leydell	L1	420
22	C. Ingin	I1	260
		S2	1,330

Sales Returns Book

Folio 8/1

19X8		Folio	£
Jan. 26	C. Ingin	I1	28
		S3	28

Purchases Day Book

Folio 8/1

19X8		Folio	£
Jan. 8	A. Hargreaves	H1	460
30	J. Gilpin	G2	220
		P1	680

19X8			Dis-count £	Cash £	Bank £	19X8			Dis-count £	Cash £	Bank £
Jan. 1	Balance b/d			200		Jan. 1	Balance b/d				6,800
11	Sales	S2		320		12	Bank	¢		200	
12	Cash	¢			200		Wages	W1		120	
29	E. Booth	B1	12		468	26	Wages	W1		120	
	M. Green-					29	A. Har-				
	ough	G1	9		351		greaves	H1			260
31	Balance c/d				6,041	31	Balance c/d			80	
		D1	21	520	7,060					520	7,060
Feb. 1	Balance b/d			80		Feb. 1	Balance b/d				6,041

Note

¢ is the abbreviation for a contra entry.

Ledger

Freehold premises   F1

19X8		£		
Jan. 1 Balance b/d		25,000		

Fittings   F2

19X8			£	19X8		£
Jan. 1	Balance b/d		12,000	Jan. 31 Balance c/d		13,200
18	N. Barrow	J8/1	1,200			
			13,200			13,200
Feb. 1	Balance b/d		13,200			

Stock   S1

19X8	£		
Jan. 1 Balance b/d	8,000		

E. Booth   B1

19X8			£	19X8		£
				Jan. 29 Cash and		
Jan. 1	Balance b/d		480	discount	CB8/1	480
2	Sales	SDB8/1	290			

35

M. Greenough   G1

19X8		£	19X8		£
Jan. 1 Balance b/d		360	Jan. 29 Cash and discount	CB8/1	360
5 Sales	SDB8/1	360			

Loan – J. Buckle   B2

			19X8		£
			Jan. 1 Balance b/d		10,000

A. Hargreaves   H1

19X8		£	19X8		£
Jan. 29 Cash	CB8/1	260	Jan. 1 Balance b/d		260
			Jan. 8 Purchases	PDB8/1	460

Provision for depreciation on fittings   F2

	19X8		£
	Jan. 1 Balance b/d		3,000

Capital   C1

	19X8		£
	Jan. 1 Balance b/d		25,980

N. Barrow   B3

	19X8		£
	Jan. 18 Fittings	J8/1	1,200

C. Leydell   L1

19X8		£
Jan. 14 Sales	SDB8/1	420

C. Ingin   I1

19X8		£	19X8		£
Jan. 22 Sales	SDB8/1	260	Jan. 26 Sales returns	SRB8/1	28
			31 Balance c/d		232
		260			260
Feb. 1 Balance b/d		232			

J. Gilpin   G2

	19X8		£
	Jan. 30 Purchases	PDB8/1	220

Sales   S2

19X8		£	19X8		£
Jan. 31 Balance c/d		1,650	Jan. 11 Cash	CB8/1	320
			31 Sales	SDB8/1	1,330
		1,650			1,650
			Feb. 1 Balance b/d		1,650

Sales returns   S3

19X8		£	
Jan. 31 Sales returns	SRB8/1	28	

Purchases   P1

19X8		£	
Jan. 31 Purchases	PDB8/1	680	

Wages   W1

19X8		£	19X8	£
Jan. 12 Cash	CB8/1	120	Jan. 31 Balance c/d	240
26 Cash	CB8/1	120		
		240		240
Feb. 1 Balance b/d		240		

Discount allowed   D1

19X8		£	
Jan. 31 Discount allowed	CB8/1	21	

37

Trial Balance at 1 February 19X8

Account no.	Name	Dr. £	Cr. £
F1	Freehold premises	25,000	
F2	Fittings	13,200	
S1	Stock	8,000	
B1	E. Booth	290	
G1	N. Greenough	360	
B2	Loan – J. Buckle		10,000
H1	A. Hargreaves		460
F2	Provision for depreciation on fittings		3,000
C1	Capital		25,980
B3	N. Barrow		1,200
L1	C. Leydell	420	
I1	C. Ingin	232	
G2	J. Gilpin		220
S2	Sales		1,650
S3	Sales returns	28	
P1	Purchases	680	
W1	Wages	240	
D1	Discount allowed	21	
CB8/1	Cash	80	
CB8/1	Bank		6,041
		48,551	48,551

For reference purposes, the books of prime entry have all been given the folio 8/1, i.e. the year and the first month of the year. In the ledger accounts, the origin of the entry can be traced from the abbreviations of the book of prime entry, e.g. Journal – J8/1.

The ledger accounts have been raised in the order of the entries in the books of prime entry starting with the journal. They have been given an alphanumeric folio, again in the order in which they are shown, e.g. Freehold premises F1, Fittings F2, Stock S1, etc.

7 Bad debts; discounts on debtors

Journal

	Dr. £	Cr. £
Bad debts account	630	
Sundry debtors account		630
Writing off of sundry bad debts.		
Profit and loss account	630	
Bad debts account		630
Transfer of balance on account.		
Provision for doubtful debts account	113	
Profit and loss account		113
Transfer of provision no longer required.		

Ledger
Provision for doubtful debts

19X5	£	19X5	£
Dec. 31 Profit and loss	113	Jan. 1 Balance b/d	725
Balance c/d	612		
	725		725
		19X6	
		Jan. 1 Balance b/d	612

Bad debts

19X5	£	19X5	£
Dec. 31 Sundry debtors	630	Dec. 31 Profit and loss	630

39

Sundry debtors

19X5		£	19X5		£
Dec. 31 Balance b/d		12,870	Dec. 31 Bad debts		630
				Balance c/d	12,240
		12,870			12,870
19X6					
Jan. 1 Balance b/d		12,240			

Workings
Provision for doubtful debts

	£
Balance at 1 January 19X5	725
Provision required at 31 December 19X5	
5% × £12,240	612
Balance – credit to profit and loss account	113

7.2S

W. Charnock
Provision for doubtful debts

19X7		£	19X7		£
Dec. 31 Profit and loss		350	Jan. 1 Balance b/d		1,400
	Balance c/d	1,050			
		1,400			1,400
19X8			19X8		
Dec. 31 Balance c/d		1,205	Jan. 1 Balance b/d		1,050
			Dec. 31 Profit and loss		155
		1,205			1,205
			19X9		
			Jan. 1 Balance b/d		1,205

Bad debts

19X7		£	19X7		£
Dec. 31 Sundry debtors		1,840	Dec. 31 Profit and loss		1,840
19X8			19X8		
Dec. 31 Sundry debtors		1,410	Dec. 31 Profit and loss		1,410

7.3S (a)

R. Young & Co.
Provision for doubtful debts

19X8	£	19X8	£
Dec. 31 Balance c/d	4,380	Jan. 1 Balance b/d	4,200
		Dec. 31 Profit and loss	180
	4,380		4,380
		19X9	
		Jan. 1 Balance b/d	4,380

(b)   Provision for discounts allowable

		19X8	£
		Dec. 31 Profit and loss	1,971

(c)   *Profit and Loss Account*
for the year ended 31 December 19X8 (extract)

	£
Expenses	
Bad debts	1,200
Provision for doubtful debts	180
Provision for discounts allowable	1,971

Workings
1. Increase in provision for doubtful debts

	£
Sundry debtors before adjustment	45,000
less Bad debts	1,200
	43,800
Provision at 10% × £43,800	4,380
less Balance at 1 January 19X8	4,200
Charge for year	180

2. Provision for discounts allowable

	£
Sundry debtors after adjustment for bad debts	43,800
less Provision for doubtful debts	4,380
	39,420
Provision at 5% × £39,420	1,971

T. O'Keefe
Discount receivable

19X1		£	19X1		£
Jan.	1 Provision b/d	600	Dec. 31 Sundry creditors	3,800
	Profit and loss	3,820		Provision c/d	620
		4,420			4,420

19X2		
Jan.	1 Provision b/d	620

Profit and Loss Account
for the year ended 31 December 19X1 (extract)

	£
Receipts	
Discount receivable	3,820

S. Urban
Trading and Profit and Loss Account
for the year ended 31 March 19X3

	£	£	£
Sales			83,580
less Sales returns			220
			83,360
Cost of goods sold			
Opening stock		18,400	
Purchases	60,080		
less Purchase returns	240	59,840	
		78,240	
less Closing stock		20,800	57,440
Gross profit			25,920
add Discounts received			1,840
			27,760
less Expenses			
Wages		10,700	
Salaries		3,500	
Lighting and heating		836	
Rent, rates and insurance		1,720	
Printing, stationery and advertising		112	
Discount allowed		2,520	
Bad debts		900	
Provision for doubtful debts		200	
Accountancy charges		656	
Depreciation on office furniture		125	21,269
Net profit			6,491

Note
Rent, rates and insurance

	£
Per trial balance	1,600
add Rent accrued	200
	1,800
less Insurance prepaid	80
Profit and loss account	1,720

Balance Sheet as at 31 March 19X3

Assets

	Cost £	Depreciation £	Net £
Fixed assets			
Freehold premises	15,440	–	15,440
Office furniture	2,500	625	1,875
	17,940	625	17,315

Current assets		
Stock	20,800	
Debtors	12,880	
Cash at bank	10,084	
Cash in hand	340	
	44,104	
less Current liabilities		
Creditors	12,068	
Working capital		32,036
		49,351

Financed by	
Capital	
Balance at 1 April 19X2	45,860
add Profit for the year	6,491
	52,351
less Drawings	3,000
	49,351

Notes
1. Debtors

	£
Per trial balance	14,400
less Provision for doubtful debts	1,600
	12,800
add Insurance prepaid	80
Balance sheet	12,880

2. Creditors

	£
Per trial balance	11,868
add Rent accrued due	200
Balance sheet	12,068

8 Control accounts

8.1S (a) The sources from which a creditors control account would be compiled are

Credits

Purchase day book	Purchases
Journal	Correction of errors

Debits

Purchase returns book	Purchase returns
Cash book	Cash paid and discounts received
Journal	Contra entries and correction of errors

(b)
Debtors control account

19X5		£	19X6		£
Jul. 1	Balance b/d	32,170	Jun. 30	Sales returns	2,640
19X6				Cash received	290,040
Jun. 30	Sales	293,220		Discounts allowed	6,740
				Bad debts written off	3,200
				Balance c/d	22,770
		325,390			325,390
Jul. 1	Balance b/d	22,770			

8.2S
S. Oldham & Co.
Sales Ledger Control account

19X8		£	19X8		£
Jan. 1	Balance b/d	20,400	Jan. 1	Balance b/d	560
Jun. 30	Sales	126,400	Jun. 30	Cash received	119,390
	Balance c/d	730		Discount allowed	3,840
				Sales returns	480
				Bad debts written off	402
				Contra entry	834
				Balance c/d	22,024
		147,530			147,530
Jul. 1	Balance b/d	22,024	Jul. 1	Balance b/d	730

Purchase ledger control account

19X8		£	19X8		£
Jan. 1	Balance b/d	120	Jan. 1	Balance b/d	14,680
Jun. 30	Cash paid	93,856	Jun. 30	Purchases	98,550
	Discounts received	2,580		Balance c/d	126
	Purchase returns	1,630			
	Contra entry	834			
	Balance c/d	14,336			
		113,356			113,356
Jul. 1	Balance b/d	126	Jul. 1	Balance b/d	14,336

8.3S (a)

Tipper
Reconciliation Statement
(adjustment to schedule of creditors)

		£	£
Original balance of schedule			12,560
add (4) Credit balances omitted		480	
(5) Cash purchase of goods wrongly dealt with		8	488
			13,048
deduct (1) Debit balance listed as credit (2 × £40)		80	
(4) Debit balances omitted		24	104
Corrected balance per purchase ledger control			12,944

(b) Purchase ledger control account

19X7		£	19X7		£
Mar. 31	Goods returned to Hector (2)	90	Mar. 31	Balance b/d (derived)	13,014
	Purchases overcast (3)	100		Contra entry – Harrow (6)	120
	Balance c/d	12,944			
		13,134			13,134
			Apr. 1	Balance b/d	12,944

46

8.4S (a)

Starling
Journal

	Dr. £	Cr. £
(1) B. Brown	20	
A. Brown		20
Correction of posting to wrong account.		
(4) Austin – Sales ledger account	60	
Sales returns		60
Cancellation of incorrect entry.		
Purchase returns	60	
Austin – Purchase ledger account		60
Credit for goods returned disallowed.		
(5) Cook – Sales ledger account	90	
Cook – Purchase ledger account		90
Contra entry not recorded in journal.		
(7) Purchases	3	
Brook – Purchase ledger account		3
Cash purchase posted incorrectly to		
Purchase ledger.		

(b)   Purchase ledger control account

19X4		£	19X4		£
Mar. 31	Purchase returns (2)	84	Mar. 31	Balance b/d	
31	Balance c/d	6,289		(derived)	6,123
				Purchase returns	
				disallowed (4)	60
				Contra entry –	
				Cook (5)	90
				Purchases	
				undercast (6)	100
		6,373			6,373
			Apr. 1	Balance b/d	6,289

Workings

Adjustment to schedule of creditors

	£	£
Original balance of schedule		5,676
add (3) Credit balances omitted	562	
(4) Increase in ledger account of Austin	60	
(7) Correction of balance – Brook	3	625
		6,301
deduct (3) Debit balances omitted		12
Corrected balance per purchase ledger control		6,289

(a)   Sales ledger control account

19X4		£	19X4			£
Jan. 1	Balance b/d	8,952	Jan./			
Jan./			Dec.	Bank		69,471
Dec.	Sales	74,753		Discounts allowed		1,817
			Dec. 31	Balance c/d		12,417
		83,705				83,705
Dec. 31	Balance b/d	12,417	Dec. 31	Bank-credit		
	Transfer to car			transfers (i)		198
	account (v)	1,173		Journal entries:		
				Contra items		
				(ii)		2,896
				Bad debts		
				written off (ii)		640
				Balance c/d		9,856
		13,590				13,590
19X5						
Jan. 1	Balance b/d	9,856				

(b)   *Reconciliation Statement*
                              (adjustment to schedule of debtors)

			£	£
Original balance of schedule				9,663
add	(iii)	Debit balances omitted	191	
	(iv)	Balance incorrectly picked up	200	391
				10,054
deduct	(i)	Credit transfers omitted		198
Corected balance per sales ledger control				9,856

(c) The benefits that accrue from operating control accounts are
    (i) Errors are localised.
   (ii) Delay in producing final accounts is reduced because work
      is able to be carried out on a number of ledgers at the same
      time.
  (iii) The system of internal control is strengthened.
  (iv) There is immediate access to totals of debtors and creditors.

9 Bank reconciliation

9.1S

Bank Reconciliation Statement
as at 31 December 19X6

	£	
Balance per cash book	6,870	In hand
add Cheques not yet presented for payment	2,560	
	9,430	In hand
deduct Lodgments not yet recorded by bank	1,510	
Balance per bank statement	7,920	In hand

9.2S (i)

Cash book

19X2		£	19X2		£
Jun. 30	Balance c/d	356	Jun. 30	Balance b/d	262
				Bank charges	94
		356			356
			Jul. 1	Balance b/d	356

(ii)

Bank Reconciliation Statement
as at 30 June 19X2

	£	£	
Balance per cash book		356	Overdrawn
deduct Cheques not yet presented			
C Limited	727		
D Limited	641		
E Limited	218	1,586	
		1,230	In hand
deduct Lodgment not yet recorded by bank		184	
Balance per bank statement		1,046	In hand

9.3S (a)
A Phillips
Cash book (bank columns)

19X1		£	19X1		£
Dec. 30	Balance b/d	461	Dec. 30	Debtor – cheque dishonoured	73
	Dividends received	38		Bank interest and charges	42
				Trade subscription	10
				Balance c/d	374
		499			499
19X2					
Jan. 1	Balance b/d	374			

(b)
Bank Reconciliation Statement
as at 30 December 19X1

	£	
Balance per cash book	374	In hand
add Cheques not yet presented	630	
	1,004	In hand
deduct Lodgments not yet recorded by bank	250	
	754	
deduct Cheque charged in error (confirmed with bank)	27	
Balance per bank statement	727	In hand

9.4S *Tutorial notes*

The question should be tackled as follows:

1. Reconcile the balances at 1 December

	£
Balance per bank statement	1,011
Balance per cash book	985
Difference	26

Since there is one cheque debited in the bank statement for the exact amount of the difference, it is safe to assume that it is that cheque which accounts for the difference. Tick the figure of £26 on the bank statement.

2. Check the items in the cash book against items on the bank statement by ticking common entries. Note that debits in the cash book have been shown individually, but all cheques banked on a particular date are shown in one total figure on the bank statement.

3. Update the cash book by recording items shown on the bank statement and not recorded in the cash book, viz.

Cash book

19X5	£	19X5	£
Dec. 31 Dividends received	1,608	Dec. 31 Balance b/d	347
		Charges	531
		Balance c/d	730
	1,608		1,608
19X6			
Jan. 1 Balance b/d	730		

4. Prepare the bank reconciliation statement.

Bank Reconciliation Statement as at 31 December 19X5

	£	£	
Balance per cash book		730	In hand
add Cheques not yet presented			
Dec. 9 J & Sons	1,060		
Dec. 22 U & Sons	247		
Dec. 22 W & Sons	431		
Dec. 29 N Associates	65		
Dec. 30 P & Q	234		
Dec. 31 D Limited	1,145		
Dec. 31 L Limited	93		
Dec. 31 E Associates	162	3,437	
Balance per bank statement		4,167	In hand

9.5S

Cash book

(a) (i) 19X7	£	19X7	£
Jun. 30 Balance b/d	3,856	Jun. 30 A. Jones – dishonoured cheque	48
Cheque received understated	100	Bank interest	10
		Balance c/d	3,898
	3,956		3,956
Jul. 1 Balance b/d	3,898		

Bank Reconciliation Statement
as at 30 June 19X7

	£	
Balance per cash book	3,898	In hand
add Cheques not yet presented	218	
	4,116	In hand
deduct Lodgment not yet recorded by bank	50	
	4,066	In hand
add Cheque credited in error by bank	95	
Balance per bank statement	4,161	In hand

(b) The basic reasons for preparing a bank reconciliation statement are to provide an independent check on the validity and accuracy of the transactions recorded in the cash book of the business.
1. *Validity*   The bank statement provides an independent check on the validity of the entries shown in the cash book and provides an independent verification of the balance shown by the cash book at the end of the period.
2. *Accuracy*   By comparing the items posted in the cash book with the bank statement, any errors can be identified, explained and corrected.

10 Partnership

10.1S   *Hayton and Co.*

		£	£
Net profit			18,000
			=====
Appropriation of profit			
Interest allowed on capital			
Hayton		600	
Webster		300	900

Share of remaining profits			
Hayton ½		8,550	
Webster ½		8,550	17,100
		-----	-----
			18,000
			=====

Current accounts

19X6		Hayton £	Webster £	19X6			Hayton £	Webster £
Dec. 31	Drawings	6,000	5,000	Jan.	1	Balance		
	Balance					b/d	1,500	200
	c/d	4,650	4,050	Dec. 31		Interest on		
						capital	600	300
						Profits	8,550	8,550
		10,650	9,050				10,650	9,050
		=====	=====				=====	=====
				19X7				
				Jan.	1	Balance		
						b/d	4,650	4,050

Tilson and Hewitt
Trading and Profit and Loss Account
for the year ended 31 March 19X7

	£	£
Sales		78,000
Cost of goods sold		
Opening stock	4,950	
Purchases	36,750	
	41,700	
less Closing stock	4,050	37,650
Gross profit		40,350
less Expenses		
Wages	3,300	
Rent and rates	8,550	
Heating and lighting	1,200	
Depreciation on shop fittings	1,500	
Depreciation on motor vans	2,250	16,800
Net profit		23,550
Appropriation of profit		
Salaries		
Tilson	7,500	
Hewitt	10,500	18,000
Interest on capital		
Tilson	300	
Hewitt	150	450
Share of remaining profits		
Tilson	2,550	
Hewitt	2,550	5,100
		23,550

Balance Sheet as at 31 March 19X7

Assets	Cost	Depre-ciation	Net
	£	£	£
Fixed assets			
Shop fittings	15,000	6,750	8,250
Motor vans	11,250	6,000	5,250
	26,250	12,750	13,500
Current assets			
Stock		4,050	
Debtors		2,400	
Cash at bank and in hand		1,920	
		8,370	

		£	£
less Current liabilities			
Creditors		1,320	
Working capital			7,050
			20,550

Financed by

	Tilson	Hewitt	
	£	£	£
Capital accounts	6,000	3,000	9,000

Current accounts

	Tilson	Hewitt	
Balances at 1 April 19X6	3,000	4,500	
Interest on capital	300	150	
Profit	2,550	2,550	
	5,850	7,200	
less Drawings	600	900	
	5,250	6,300	11,550
			20,550

Workings

1. Rent and rates

	£
Per trial balance	9,300
less Rent prepaid	750
	8,550

2. Debtors

	£
Per trial balance	1,650
add Rent prepaid	750
	2,400

10.3S

Hawes and Peters
Trading and Profit and Loss Account
for the year ended 31 December 19X5

	£	£
Sales		131,860
Cost of goods sold		
Opening stock	17,360	
Purchases	101,640	
	119,000	

	£	£
less Closing stock	26,380	92,620
Gross profit		39,240
add Provision for doubtful debts no longer required		180
		39,420
less Expenses		
Wages	7,730	
Rent	928	
Insurance	550	
Office expenses	6,400	
Vehicle expenses	3,560	
Bank charges	70	
Discounts allowed	2,560	
Bad debts	200	
Depreciation on fittings	126	
Depreciation on vans	1,136	
Depreciation on car	160	23,420
Net profit		16,000
Appropriation of profit		
Interest on capital		
Hawes	1,640	
Peters	1,320	2,960
Share of remaining profits		
Hawes 3/5	7,824	
Peters 2/5	5,216	13,040
		16,000

Balance Sheet as at 31 December 19X5

Assets

	Cost	Depre-ciation	Net
	£	£	£
Fixed assets			
Fittings	2,400	1,266	1,134
Vans	11,600	7,056	4,544
Motor car	1,600	320	1,280
	15,600	8,642	6,958
Current assets			
Stock		26,380	
Debtors		11,770	
Petty cash		40	
		38,190	

	£	£	£
less Current liabilities			
Creditors	5,498		
Bank	610	6,108	
Working capital			32,082
			39,040

Financed by

	Hawes	Peters	
	£	£	£
Capital accounts	16,400	13,200	29,600
Current accounts			
Interest on capital	1,640	1,320	
Profit	7,824	5,216	
	9,464	6,536	
less Drawings	4,160	2,400	
	5,304	4,136	9,440
			39,040

Workings

1. Provision for doubtful debts

	£
Debtors per trial balance	12,200
less Bad debts	200
	12,000
Provision of 2½% × £12,000	300
Existing provision	480
Credit to profit and loss	180

2. Wages

	£
Per trial balance	7,360
add Amount owing	370
	7,730

3. Insurance

	£
Per trial balance	620
less Amount prepaid	70
	550

57

4. Vehicle expenses

	£
Per trial balance	3,960
less Charged to Hawes	400
	3,560

5. Depreciation on fittings

	£
Cost	2,400
less Depreciation to 1 January 19X5	1,140
	1,260
10% × £1,260	126

6. Depreciation on vans

	£
Cost	11,600
less Depreciation to 1 January 19X5	5,920
	5,680
20% × £5,680	1,136

7. Depreciation on car

	£
20% × £1,600	320
less Charged to Hawes	160
	160

8. Debtors

	£
After writing off bad debts	12,000
less Provision for doubtful debts	300
	11,700
add Insurance prepaid	70
	11,770

9. Creditors

	£
Per trial balance	4,200
add Wages owing	370
Rent owing	928
	5,498

10. Bank

	£
Per trial balance	540
add Bank charges	70
	610

11. Hawes – drawings

	£
Per trial balance	3,600
add Vehicle expenses	400
Vehicle depreciation	160
	4,160

10.4S (a)

Rowe and Martin
Summary of adjustments to the Profit and Loss Account
for the year ended 31 December 19X9

	Add	Deduct	£
Net profit for the year (2 × £4,770)			9,540
Adjustments	£	£	
(1) Loss on sale of freehold premises		500	
(2) Net book value of plant and machinery scrapped		215	
(3) Motor vehicle licences prepaid – 6/12 × £100	50		
(4) Bad debts		291	
(5) Stocks – reduced to net realisable value		570	
Stocks – scrap metal omitted	330		
(6) Cash misappropriated		35	
	380	1,611	
		380	1,231
Adjusted net profit			8,309
Appropriation of profit			
Interest allowed on capital			
Rowe		1,629	
Martin		558	2,187
Share of remaining profits			
Rowe ½		3,061	
Martin ½		3,061	6,122
			8,309

(b) *Balance Sheet as at 31 December 19X9*

Assets

	Cost	Depre-ciation	Net
	£	£	£
Fixed assets			
Freehold buildings	11,500	–	11,500
Plant and machinery	14,385	6,600	7,785
Motor vehicles	8,000	2,700	5,300
	33,885	9,300	24,585

Current assets			
Stocks at lower of cost and net realisable value		4,760	
Debtors		13,759	
Cash at bank		762	
Cash in hand		5	
		19,286	
less Current liabilities			
Creditors		11,262	
Working capital			8,024
			32,609

Financed by

	Rowe	Martin	
	£	£	£
Capital accounts	20,100	10,000	30,100
Current accounts			
Interest on capital	1,629	558	
Profit	3,061	3,061	
	4,690	3,619	
less Drawings	2,000	3,800	
	2,690	(181)	2,509
			32,609

Tutorial note

The overdrawn balance on Martin's current account is deducted from Rowe's current account balance in the balance sheet.

Workings

1. Bad debts

	£
Debts written off	521
Provision for doubtful debts	270
	791
less Existing provision	500
	291

2. Freehold buildings

	£
Per draft accounts	12,000
less Loss on sale	500
	11,500

3. Plant and machinery – cost

	£
Per draft accounts	15,000
less Cost of plant scrapped	615
	14,385

4. Plant and machinery – depreciation

	£
Per draft accounts	7,000
less Depreciation on plant scrapped	400
	6,600

5. Stocks

	£
Per draft accounts	5,000
add Stock omitted	330
	5,330
less Stock reduced in value	570
	4,760

6. Debtors

	£
Per draft accounts	14,000
less Bad debts, etc.	291
	13,709
add Motor vehicle licences prepaid	50
	13,759

7. Cash at bank

	£
Per draft accounts – overdrawn	2,700
add Cheques not mailed	3,462
	762

8. Petty cash

	£
Per draft accounts	40
less Cash misappropriated	35
	5

9. Creditors

	£
Per draft accounts	7,800
add Cheques not mailed	3,462
	11,262

11

Goodwill, with particular reference to partnership; revaluation of assets

11.1S

Edwards and Coleman
Balance Sheet as at 1 January 19X7

Assets

	£	£
Fixed assets		21,000
Current assets	12,000	
less Current liabilities	8,000	
Net current assets		4,000
		25,000

Financed by

	Edwards £	Coleman £	£
Capital accounts	7,000	8,000	15,000
Current accounts	7,500	2,500	10,000
			25,000

Workings

Journal

	Dr. £	Cr. £
Capital account – Edwards	500	
Capital account – Coleman		500

Adjustments to capital accounts to record
the agreed value of goodwill at 31 December
19X6, on a change in profit sharing ratio: viz.

	Old ratio Cr. £	New ratio Dr. £	Net £
Edwards	2,500	3,000	500 Dr.
Coleman	2,500	2,000	500 Cr.

63

(a)   Capital accounts

	Exe £	Wye £	Zed £		Exe £	Wye £	Zed £
Cash	6,000	3,000		Balances			
Balances				b/f	24,000	12,000	
c/d	24,000	12,000	9,000	Cash from			
				Zed	6,000	3,000	9,000
	30,000	15,000	9,000		30,000	15,000	9,000
				Balances			
				b/d	24,000	12,000	9,000

(b)   *Exe, Wye, Zed*
                    Balance Sheet as at 1 April 19X6

	£	£
Assets		
Fixed assets		24,000
Current assets (excluding cash)	54,000	
Cash at bank	15,000	
	69,000	
less Current liabilities	48,000	
Net current assets		21,000
		45,000
Financed by		
Capital accounts		
Exe	24,000	
Wye	12,000	
Zed	9,000	45,000
		45,000

Tutorial note

The cash at bank will increase by the same amount as the credit shown in Zed's capital account. The balance of £9,000 introduced by Zed was withdrawn by Exe and Wye.

Doohan, Buckley and Mannion
Capital accounts

	Doohan £	Buckley £	Mannion £		Doohan £	Buckley £	Mannion £
Adjust-ments for goodwill		4,000	2,000	Balance b/d	20,000	20,000	10,000
				Goodwill	6,000		
Transfer to loan account	26,000						
Balance c/d		16,000	8,000				
	26,000	20,000	10,000		26,000	20,000	10,000
				Balance b/d		16,000	8,000

(b)   *Balance Sheet as at 1 January 19X4*

	£	£
Assets		
Fixed assets		40,800
Current assets (excluding bank)	31,300	
Cash at bank	7,750	
	39,050	
less Current liabilities	26,800	
Net current assets		12,250
		53,050

	Buckley £	Mannion £	£
Financed by			
Capital accounts	16,000	8,000	24,000
Current accounts	1,600	1,450	3,050
Loan – Doohan			26,000
			53,050

Workings

Journal

	Dr. £	Cr. £
Capital accounts – Buckley	4,000	
Mannion	2,000	
Capital account – Doohan		6,000

Adjustments to capital accounts to record
the agreed goodwill at 31 December 19X3.

	Old ratio Cr. £	New ratio Dr. £	Net £
Doohan	6,000		6,000 *Cr.*
Buckley	6,000	10,000	4,000 *Dr.*
Mannion	3,000	5,000	2,000 *Dr.*

Balance at bank

	£
Per balance sheet at 31 December 19X3	9,600
deduct Repayment of Doohan's current account balance	1,850
	7,750

11.4S (a)

Leech, Luff, Lee and Windward
Statement showing the division of profit
for the year ended 31 December 19X7

	£	£
Net profit		17,640
add Interest on current account debit balances		
Lee 8% on £792	63	
Windward 8% on £496	40	103
		17,743

Allocation of profit adjusted for interest on drawings	Leech £	Luff £	Lee £	Windward £	Total £
Interest on capital	1,080	540	180	180	1,980
Salary				1,500	1,500
Remaining profit					
3 : 3 : 3 : 1	4,279	4,279	4,279	1,426	14,263
	5,359	4,819	4,459	3,106	17,743
Adjustment for					
guarantee	(74)			74	
	5,285	4,819	4,459	3,180	17,743

(b) <center>Current accounts</center>

	Leech £	Luff £	Lee £	Wind-ward £		Leech £	Luff £	Lee £	Wind-ward £
Goodwill in new profit-sharing ratios	2,988	2,988	2,988	996	Balance b/f	5,000	1,000	1,200	
Balance c/d	7,988	1,000			Cash introduced				500
					Goodwill in old profit-sharing ratios	5,976	2,988	996	
					Balance c/d			792	496
	10,976	3,988	2,988	996		10,976	3,988	2,988	996
Balance b/d			792	496	Balance b/d	7,988	1,000		
Interest on current a/c			63	40	Profit	5,285	4,819	4,459	3,180
Drawings	6,320	4,900	4,900	2,193	Balance c/d			1,296	
Balance c/d	6,953	919		451					
	13,273	5,819	5,755	3,180		13,273	5,819	5,755	3,180
Balance b/d			1,296		Balance b/d	6,953	919		451

Notes
1. To determine the balances on the partners' current accounts at 1 January 19X7, the first part of requirement (b) must be prepared first.
2. It has been assumed that interest on capital is to be ignored in determining Windward's guaranteed aggregate of salary and share of profits of £3,000.

Workings

Valuation of Goodwill

	£	£
Profits, year ended 31 December:		
19X6	16,337	16,337
19X5	10,255	10,255
19X4	10,758	10,758
19X3	–	14,164
	37,350	51,514
Average	£12,450	£12,878
Goodwill is, therefore, 80% × £12,450	£9,960	

11.5S (a)

Colours
Trading and Profit and Loss Account
for the year ended 30 September 19X2

	£	£
Sales		96,000
Cost of goods sold		
Opening stock	12,400	
Purchases	62,000	
	74,400	
less Closing stock	14,200	60,200
Gross profit		35,800

	Half year to 31 March 19X2		Half year to 30 September 19X2	
	£	£	£	£
Gross profit allocated on time basis		17,900		17,900
less Expenses				
Wages	7,300		7,300	
Salaries	3,450		2,250	
Trade expenses	765		1,015	
Rent and rates	500		500	
Bad debts	600			
Bad debts provision			230	
Depreciation:				
Plant and machinery	700		700	
Motor vehicles	775		600	
Interest on loan			540	
		14,090		13,135
		3,810		4,765

	£	£	£	£
Appropriation of profit				
Interest on capital				
Brown	240			
Green	180		84	
Black			96	
	———	420	———	180
Remaining profits				
Brown	2,260			
Green	1,130		2,751	
Black			1,834	
	———	3,390	———	4,585
		3,810		4,765

(b) Capital accounts

	Brown £	Green £	Black £		Brown £	Green £	Black £
Goodwill in new ratios		7,200	4,800	Balances b/f	8,000	6,000	
Transfer to loan account	16,000			Goodwill in old ratios	8,000	4,000	
Balances c/d		2,800	3,200	Cash – introduced			3,000
				paid to Brown			5,000
	16,000	10,000	8,000		16,000	10,000	8,000
				Balances b/d		2,800	3,200

Current accounts

	Brown £	Green £	Black £		Brown £	Green £	Black £
Car taken over	600			Balances b/f	2,400	1,600	
Drawings	1,800	2,400	900	Interest on capital	240	264	96
Transfer to loan account	2,500			Profit	2,260	3,881	1,834
Balances c/d		3,345	1,030				
	4,900	5,745	1,930		4,900	5,745	1,930
				Balances b/d		3,345	1,030

Balance Sheet as at 30 September 19X2

Assets	Cost	Depre-ciation	Net
	£	£	£
Fixed assets			
Plant and machinery	14,000	4,200	9,800
Motor vehicles	4,800	3,975	825
	18,800	8,175	10,625
Current assets			
Stock		14,200	
Debtors		4,770	
Balance at bank		1,200	
		20,170	
less Current liabilities			
Creditors		6,380	
Net current assets			13,790
			24,415

Financed by	Green	Black	
	£	£	£
Capital accounts	2,800	3,200	6,000
Current accounts	3,345	1,030	4,375
Loan – Brown			14,040
			24,415

Workings
1. Salaries

	£	£
Total per trial balances		10,800
Deduct: Partners drawings – Brown	1,800	
Green	2,400	
Black	900	5,100
		5,700

Allocation:	£
Half-year to 31 March 19X2:	
$\frac{1}{2} \times$ (£5,700 − £1,200) + Black's salary of £1,200 =	3,450
Half-year to 30 September 19X2:	
$\frac{1}{2} \times$ (£5,700 − £1,200) =	2,250
	5,700

2. Trade expenses

	£
Total per trial balance	1,600
add Accrual	180
	1,780

Allocation:

	£
Half-year to 31 March 19X2:	
$\frac{1}{2} \times$ (£1,780 − £250)	765
Half-year to 30 September 19X2:	
$\frac{1}{2} \times$ (£1,780 − £250) + professional charges of £250	1,015
	1,780

3. Rent and rates

	£
Total per trial balance	1,400
deduct Rent paid in advance	400
	1,000

Allocation: 50 : 50

4. Depreciation
Plant and machinery
   10% per annum on £14,000 = £1,400   Allocated 50 : 50
Motor vehicles
   Half-year to 31 March 19X2: 25% per annum on £6,200 = £775
   Half-year to 30 September 19X2: 25% per annum on £4,800 = £600

5. Loan account and interest – Brown

	£		£
Cash from Black	5,000	Transfer from capital	
Balance c/d	14,040	account	16,000
		Transfer from current	
		account	2,500
		Profit and loss account	
		Interest at 8% p.a. on	
		£13,500 for six months	540
	19,040		19,040
		Balance b/d	14,040

71

6. Car taken over by Brown

	£	£
Cost		1,400
Depreciation – to 30 September 19X1	625	
to 31 March 19X2	175	800
		600

7. Motor vehicles

	Cost £	Depreciation £
Per trial balance	6,200	3,400
less Vehicle sold	1,400	800
	4,800	2,600
Charge for year to 30 September 19X2		1,375
		3,975

8. Debtors

	£
Balance per trial balance	4,600
add Rent prepaid	400
	5,000
less Provision for bad debts	230
	4,770

9. Creditors

	£
Balance per trial balance	6,200
add Trade expenses accrued	180
	6,380

11.6S (a)

Lock, Stock and Barrel
Revaluation account

	£	£		£
Plant and equipment		700	Freehold premises	7,000
Motor vehicle taken			Goodwill	7,000
over by Lock		50		
Capital accounts:				
Lock (5)	6,625			
Stock (3)	3,975			
Barrel (2)	2,650	13,250		
		14,000		14,000

(b)   Capital accounts

	Lock £	Stock £	Barrel £		Lock £	Stock £	Barrel £
Adjustments to profit for year ended 30 June 19X3	475	285	190	Balances b/d	12,000	6,000	4,000
Car taken over	400			Profit on revaluation	6,625	3,975	2,650
Goodwill written off		4,200	2,800				
Transfer to loan account	17,750						
Balances c/d		5,490	3,660				
	18,625	9,975	6,650		18,625	9,975	6,650
				Balances b/d		5,490	3,660

(c)   Lock – loan account

	£		£
Repaid	3,000	Balance b/d	3,000
Balances c/d		Transferred from	
Current liability 10%	1,775	capital account	17,750
Deferred liability 90%	15,975		
	20,750		20,750
		Balances b/d	
		Current liability	1,775
		Deferred liability	15,975

(d)   *Stock and Barrel*
                      Balance Sheet as at 1 July 19X3

	£	£	£
Assets			
Fixed assets at valuation on 30 June 19X3			
Freehold premises			15,000
Plant and equipment			3,500
Motor vehicles			1,650
			20,150
Current assets			
Stock		3,200	
Debtors		4,600	
Balance at bank		5,300	
		13,100	

	£	£	£
less Current liabilities			
Creditors	4,350		
Provision for repainting of premises	2,000		
Loan – Lock	1,775	8,125	
Net current assets			4,975
			25,125

Financed by	Stock	Barrel	
	£	£	£
Capital accounts	5,490	3,660	9,150
Loan – Lock			15,975
			25,125

Note

It has been assumed that the 10% of the outstanding balance on Lock's loan account had not been repaid at 1 July 19X3.

Workings

1. Adjustment of profit 19X3

Per draft accounts			£ 8,150
	Add	*Deduct*	
	£	£	
(3) Increase in provision for doubtful debts		200	
(4) Increase in provision for repainting		600	
(5) Damaged and obsolete stock		400	
(6) Creditors provision written back	250		
	250	1,200	
		250	950
Adjusted profit			7,200

Apportionment of reduction in profit

		£
Lock	50%	475
Stock	30%	285
Barrel	20%	190
		950

2. Goodwill

	£	£
Profits year ended 30 June		
19X9		6,420
19X0		5,360
19X1	8,180	8,180
19X2	7,840	7,840
19X3	7,200	7,200
	23,220	35,000
Average	7,740	7,000
Goodwill		7,000

3. Motor vehicles

	£
Per draft balance sheet	2,100
less Book value of vehicle taken over by Lock	450
	1,650

4. Debtors

	£
Per draft balance sheet	5,200
less Provision for doubtful debts	600
	4,600

5. Balance at bank

	£
Per draft balance sheet	8,300
less Payment to Lock	3,000
	5,300

6. Creditors

	£
Per draft balance sheet	4,600
less Provision no longer required	250
	4,350

12 Partnership dissolution

12.1S (a)

Anderson and Birch
Realisation account

	£			£
Plant and machinery	8,500	Cash – sale of assets		14,000
Stock	4,900	Creditors – discount		124
Debtors	4,100	Loss on realisation:		
Cash – realisation expenses	300	Anderson	1,838	
		Birch	1,838	3,676
	17,800			17,800

(b)

Cash account

	£			£
Balance b/d	1,600	Creditors		2,976
Realisation of assets	14,000	Realisation account – costs		300
		Capital accounts:		
		Anderson	6,162	
		Birch	6,162	12,324
	15,600			15,600

(c)

Capital accounts

	Anderson £	Birch £		Anderson £	Birch £
Realisation – loss	1,838	1,838	Balances b/d	8,000	8,000
Cash	6,162	6,162			
	8,000	8,000		8,000	8,000

Old and Young
Realisation account

	£			£
Warehouse	50,000	Old capital account –		
Retail shops	75,000	(warehouse + warehouse		
Fixtures	15,000	stock)		80,000
Motor vehicles	8,400	Young capital account –		
Stocks	75,000	(retail shops + shops'		
Debtors	2,400	stock + fixtures)		136,500
Cash – dissolution costs	1,200	Cash – motor vehicles		8,000
		Cash – debtors		2,400
		Loss on realisation:		
		Old	67	
		Young	33	100
	227,000			227,000

Cash account

	£		£
Balance b/d	2,700	Creditors	17,800
Realisation account		Realisation account –	
Sale of motor vehicles	8,000	dissolution costs	1,200
Debtors	2,400	Capital account – Old	60,193
Capital account – Young	66,093		
	79,193		79,193

Capital accounts

	Old £	Young £		Old £	Young £
Realisation account – assets taken over	80,000	136,500	Balances b/d	75,000	50,000
			Transfer from current account	25,260	20,440
Loss on realisation	67	33	Transfer from loan account	40,000	
Cash	60,193		Cash		66,093
	140,260	136,533		140,260	136,533

12.3S (a)　　　　　　　　*Smart and Swift*
　　　Profit and Loss Account for the year ended 31 December 19X8

	£	£	£
Hotel takings			5,100
less Expenses			
Foodstuffs – Stock at 31 December 19X7	420		
Purchases	2,600		
	3,020		
less Stock at 31 December 19X8	300	2,720	
Wages		2,200	
General expenses		870	
Depreciation on motor vehicle		200	
Depreciation on fittings and fixtures		100	
Loan interest – Smart		180	6,270
Net loss			1,170
Divided:			
Smart – 3/5ths			702
Swift – 2/5ths			468
			1,170

(b)　　　　　　　　　　Realisation account

	£			£	£
Freehold premises	6,000	Smart's capital account			
Fittings and fixtures	1,700	Stock	250		
Motor vehicle	500	Fittings and			
Stock	300	fixtures (part)	600		
Debtors	600	Sundry items	40	890	
Cash – dissolution					
expenses	120	Swift's capital account			
Profit on realisation·		Motor vehicle	400		
Smart (3/5) 462		Sundry items	20	420	
Swift (2/5) 308	770				
		Cash – freehold premises		6,800	
		Cash – debtors		480	
		Cash – fittings and			
		fixtures		1,400	
	9,990			9,990	

(c)

Cash account for January 19X9

	£		£
Realisation account		Balance b/d	4,590
Sale of freehold		Creditors	270
premises	6,800	Realisation account –	
Debtors	480	dissolution expenses	120
Sale of fittings and		Capital account – Smart	4,530
fixtures	1,400		
Capital account – Swift	830		
	9,510		9,510

(d)

Capital accounts

	Smart £	Swift £		Smart £	Swift £
Drawings	520	750	Balances b/d	3,000	500
Net loss for 19X8	702	468	Transfer from loan		
Realisation account –			account	3,000	
assets taken over	890	420	Loan interest	180	
Cash	4,530		Profit on realisation	462	308
			Cash		830
	6,642	1,638		6,642	1,638

12.4S

Clark, Hibbert and Thomas
Realisation account

	£			£
Fixtures and fittings	2,000	Cash – sale of stock		6,800
Stock	9,000	debtors		4,650
Debtors	5,000	sale of fixtures		1,700
Cash – realisation		Creditors – discount received		100
expenses	400	Loss – capital accounts		
		Clark	1,050	
		Hibbert	1,050	
		Thomas	1,050	3,150
	16,400			16,400

Cash account

	£			£
Balance b/d	2,500	Creditors		7,150
Realisation account		Realisation expenses		400
Sale of stock	6,800	Capital accounts		
Debtors	4,650	Clark	4,900	
Sale of fixtures	1,700	Thomas	3,200	8,100
	15,650			15,650

Capital accounts

	Clark £	Hibbert £	Thomas £		Clark £	Hibbert £	Thomas £
Balance b/d		750		Balance b/d	7,000		5,000
Loss on realisation	1,050	1,050	1,050	Deficiency shared by Clark and			
Hibbert's deficiency	1,050		750	Thomas		1,800	
Cash	4,900		3,200				
	7,000	1,800	5,000		7,000	1,800	5,000

Note

The loss on realisation is shared between all three partners in their profit sharing ratios: Hibbert's total deficiency is then borne by Clark and Thomas in the ratio of their last agreed capital account balances.

13 Manufacturing accounts

13.1S (a)

N. Jones
Manufacturing, Trading and Profit and Loss Account
for the year ended 30 April 19X1

	£	£
Sales		220,000
Cost of sales		
Materials consumed (Note 1)	80,000	
Manufacturing wages	40,000	
	———	
Prime cost	120,000	
Manufacturing expenses	20,800	
Depreciation (Note 2)	9,600	
Work in progress, 1 May 19X0	6,300	
	———	
	156,700	
less Work in progress, 30 April 19X1	6,300	
	———	
Manufacturing cost	150,400	
Stock of finished goods, 1 May 19X0	43,000	
	———	
	193,400	
less Stock of finished goods, 30 April 19X1	39,000	154,400
	———	———
Gross profit		65,600
Selling and distribution expenses (Note 3)	24,050	
Administration expenses (Note 4)	15,250	39,300
	———	———
Net profit		26,300
		════

Balance Sheet as at 30 April 19X1

Assets

	Cost	Depre-ciation	Net
	£	£	£
Fixed assets	120,000	60,000	60,000
	════	════	

81

	Cost £	Depreciation £	Net £
Current assets			
Stock and work in progress (Note 5)		55,300	
Debtors (Note 6)		28,700	
Cash at bank and in hand		9,000	
		93,000	
less Current liabilities			
Creditors (Note 7)		9.900	
Net current assets			83,100
			143,100
Financed by			
Capital account			105,000
Current account			
Balance at 1 May 19X0		21,800	
add Profit for the year		26,300	
		48,100	
less Drawings		10,000	38,100
			143,100

(b) 'Direct' means that the materials, labour and expenses involved in the manufacturing process are *traceable* to the particular unit of goods being made.

Notes

1. Materials consumed

	£
Stock at 1 May 19X0	8,000
Purchases	82,000
	90,000
less Stock at 30 April 19X1	10,000
	80,000

2. Depreciation

		£
10% × £120,000	=	12,000
Manufacturing 8/10	=	9,600
Selling and distribution 1/10	=	1,200
Administration 1/10	=	1,200
		12,000

3. Selling and distribution expenses

	£
Per trial balance	21,400
Bad debts written off	600
Increase in provision for doubtful debts	250
Depreciation	1,200
Accruals at 30 April 19X1	700
	24,150
less Prepayment at 30 April 19X1	100
	24,050

4. Administration expenses

	£
Per trial balance	13,950
Depreciation	1,200
Accruals at 30 April 19X1	200
	15,350
less Prepayment at 30 April 19X1	100
	15,250

5. Stock and work in progress at 30 April 19X1

	£
Materials	10,000
Work-in-progress	6,300
Finished goods	39,000
	55,300

6. Debtors

		£
Per trial balance		30,600
Prepayments: Selling and distribution		100
Administration		100
		30,800
less Bad debts	600	
Provision for doubtful debts	1,500	2,100
		28,700

7. Creditors

	£
Per trial balance	9,000
Accruals: Selling and distribution	700
Administration	200
	9,900

Black and White
Manufacturing, Trading and Profit and Loss Account
for the year ended 31 December 19X5

	£	£
Sales		20,250
Cost of sales		
Materials consumed (Note 1)	3,000	
Manufacturing wages (Note 2)	5,000	
Prime cost	8,000	
Factory overhead expenses (Note 3)	2,000	
Factory cost of goods produced	10,000	
Factory profit – 2/7 × £10,000	2,857	
	12,857	
Stock of finished goods, 1 January 19X5 (Note 4)	2,572	
	15,429	
less Stock of finished goods at 31 December 19X5 (Note 4)	1,929	13,500
		6,750
Sales overhead expenses (Note 5)		2,200
Sales department profit		4,550
Factory profit		2,857
Provision for unrealised profit written back (Note 6)		143
		7,550
Allocation of profits (Note 7)		
Black		3,211
White		4,339
		7,550

(b)
Black and White
Balance Sheet as at 31 December 19X5
Assets

	Cost	Depreciation	Net
	£	£	£
Fixed assets			
Freehold factory	8,500	550	7,950
Gas ovens and factory equipment	750	375	375
Delivery vans	1,250	750	500
	10,500	1,675	8,825

	Cost	Depreciation	Net
	£	£	£
Current assets			
Stocks at cost (Note 8)		2,000	
Debtors (Note 9)		2,235	
Cash at bank		475	
		4,710	
less Current liabilities			
Creditors (Note 10)		2,175	
Net current assets			2,535
			11,360

Financed by	Black	White	Net
Capital accounts	Black	White	
Balances brought forward	3,460	4,150	
Profit for the year	3,211	4,339	
	6,671	8,489	
less Drawings	1,700	2,100	
	4,971	6,389	11,360

Notes

1. Materials consumed

	£
Stock at 1 January 19X5	750
Purchases	2,750
	3,500
less Stock at 31 December 19X5	500
	3,000

2. Manufacturing wages

	£
Wages per trial balance	6,200
less Sales department wages (2 × £600)	1,200
	5,000

3. Factory overhead expenses

	£
Gas (£700 + £300)	1,000
Rates and insurance (£225 − £50)	175
Sundry expenses	700
Depreciation:	
Factory building 2% × (£8,500 − £6,000)	50
Gas ovens, etc., 10% × £750	75
	2,000

4. Stock of finished goods

If finished goods are transferred from the factory to the sales department at cost plus two-sevenths, the factory profit must be included in the finished goods stock before the sales department profit can be calculated.

Stock of finished goods at 1 January 19X5 will be shown as
Cost + 9/7 = £2,000 + £572 = £2,572.

Stock of finished goods at 31 December 19X5 will be shown as
Cost + 9/7 = £1,500 + £429 = £1,929.

5. Sales overhead expenses

	£
Wages	1,200
Advertising (£225 + £75)	300
Delivery van running expenses (£485 − £35)	450
Depreciation on delivery vans −	
20% × £1,250	250
	2,200

6. Provision for unrealised profit written back

	£
Unrealised profit on finished goods	
Brought forward, 2/9 × £2,572	572
Carried forward, 2/9 × £1,929	429
	143

Whenever stock is shown at a figure above cost in the trading account, a provision must be made to reduce the stock to cost. Where the opening stock is greater than the closing stock, the provision required at the year end will be smaller than that required at the beginning of the year. As in this case, the provision no longer required will be written back.

7. Allocation of profits

	Black £	White £	Balance £
Factory profit – Black, 2/3 × £2,857	1,905		952
Sales department profit – White 2/3 × £4,550		3,033	1,517
Provision for unrealised profit			143
Balance allocated equally	1,306	1,306	2,612
	3,211	4,339	

8. Stock at cost

	£
Raw materials	500
Finished goods	1,500
	2,000

9. Debtors

	£
Per trial balance	2,300
Prepayments: Rates	50
Van licences	35
	2,385
less Provision for doubtful debts	150
	2,235

10. Creditors

	£
Per trial balance	1,800
Accruals: Gas	300
Advertising	75
	2,175

13.3S (a)

Field, Meadow and Park
Trading and Profit and Loss Account
for the year ended 31 December 19X2

	£	£
Sales (Note 1)		102,200
Cost of sales		
Materials consumed (Note 2)	44,200	
Manufacturing wages and bonuses	15,200	
Prime cost	59,400	
Factory overhead expenses (Note 3)	2,270	
Manufacturing cost		61,670

	£	£
Gross profit		40,530
Administration expenses (Note 4)	7,550	
Finance expenses (Note 5)	1,350	
Depreciation of motor vehicles (Note 6)	300	9,000
Net profit		31,330

Appropriation of profit	Field	Meadow	Park	Total
	£	£	£	£
Interest on capital	1,000	700	300	2,000
Share of remaining profits				
(4 : 2 : 1)	16,760	8,380	4,190	29,330
	17,760	9,080	4,490	31,330
Adjustment for Park's				
guarantee in ratio 4 : 2	(340)	(170)	510	
	17,420	8,910	5,000	31,330

(b)   *Balance Sheet as at 31 December 19X2*

Assets

	Cost	Depreciation	Net
	£	£	£
Fixed assets			
Freehold premises	22,000		22,000
Plant and machinery (Note 7)	16,000	4,860	11,740
Motor vehicles (Note 8)	2,000	900	1,100
	40,600	5,760	34,840
Current assets			
Stock (Note 9)		15,040	
Debtors (Note 10)		6,390	
Cash at bank		2,360	
		23,790	
less Current liabilities			
Creditors (Note 11)		6,800	
Net current assets			16,990
			51,830
Financed by			
Capital accounts			
Field		10,000	
Meadow		7,000	
Park		3,000	20,000

	Cost	Depre-ciation	Net
	£	£	£
Current accounts			
Field		18,620	
Meadow		9,290	
Park		3,920	31,830
			51,830

(c)   Current accounts

	Field £	Meadow £	Park £		Field £	Meadow £	Park £
Balance b/f			600	Balances b/f	2,400	1,100	
Drawings	1,200	720	480	Share of			
Balances c/d	18,620	9,290	3,920	profit	17,420	8,910	5,000
	19,820	10,010	5,000		19,820	10,010	5,000
				Balances b/d	18,620	9,290	3,920

Notes
1. Sales

	£
Per trial balance	104,000
less Goods on sale or return	1,800
(see Tutorial Note 1 p. 91)	
	102,200

2. Materials consumed

	£
Stock, 1 January 19X2	12,400
Purchases and carriage inwards	46,840
	59,240
less Stock at 31 December 19X2 (Note 9)	15.040
	44,200

3. Factory overhead expenses

	£
Repairs	1,210
less Amount capitalised	600
	610
Depreciation on plant and machinery -	
10% × £16,600	1,660
	2,270

4. Administration expenses

		£
Salaries and bonuses		
	Salaries per trial balance	6,100
	less Partners' drawings	2,400
		3,700
Bonuses		1,400
		5,100
Office expenses		2,450
		7,550

5. Finance expenses

	£
Discounts allowed	980
Bad debts written off	210
Increase in provision for doubtful debts	160
	1,350

6. Depreciation of motor vehicles

	£
Charge for year	500
less Overprovision on vehicle sold	
during the year	200
	300

7. Plant and machinery – cost

	£
Per trial balance	16,000
Repairs capitalised	600
	16,600

8. Motor vehicles

	Cost	Depreciation
	£	£
Per trial balance	3,400	1,400
deduct Sale of vehicle	1,400	1,000
	2,000	400
Depreciation for year		500
		900

9. Stock

	£	£
Stock per Note 1 to trial balance		13,600
add Stock in customers hands at selling price	1,800	
less Mark-up	360	1,440
		15,040

10. Debtors

	£	£
Per trial balance		9,400
less Goods on sale or return	1,800	
Bad debt written off	210	
Provision for doubtful debts	1,000	3,010
		6,390

11. Creditors

	£
Per trial balance	4,600
add Bonuses	2,200
	6,800

Tutorial Notes

1. When goods are sent to customers on 'sale or return', the profit should not be taken until the customer acknowledges his intention to keep the goods and pay for them. Where the goods remain unsold at the balance sheet date and they have been invoiced to customers through the normal sales procedure (as in this question), it is necessary for the sales account to be reduced by the selling price of those goods and the closing stock to be increased by the cost price of those goods. The double entries are as follows:

Sales account	Debit	
Debtors		Credit
With the selling price of the goods.		

Stock account (i.e. closing stock)	Debit	
Trading account (through the closing stock)		Credit
With the cost price of the goods.		

2. Although the question did not ask for a manufacturing account, the partners were in a manufacturing business. In such cases, it is suggested that answers should be prepared in a manufacturing format so far as the information given will allow.

14 Incomplete records

P. Jennings
Trading Account for the year ended 31 December 19X2

	£	£
Sales		24,696
deduct Cost of sales		
Opening stock	6,933	
add Purchases	16,711	
	23,644	
less Closing stock	7,180	16,464
Gross profit		8,232

Workings

In trading account form the information given would show the following:

Trading Account for the year ended 31 December 19X2

	£	£
Sales		24,696
deduct Cost of sales		
Opening stock	6,933	
add Purchases	16,711	
	23,644	
less Closing stock		
Cost of sales		
Gross profit		8,232

The two missing figures, i.e. the cost of sales and the closing stock can be deduced and inserted and the trading account completed.

G. Holt
Balance Sheet as at 31 December 19X2

				£
Capital employed				
Capital account balance as at 1 January 19X2				17,246
add Profit for the year				3,839
				21,085
deduct Drawings				3,120
				17,965

Represented by

	Cost	Depre-ciation	Net
	£	£	£
Fixed assets	20,000	10,000	10,000
Current assets			
Stock		4,838	
Debtors		2,856	
Bank		2,221	
		9,915	
deduct Current liabilities			
Trade creditors	1,568		
Expense creditors	382	1,950	
Net current assets			7,965
			17,965

Workings

In balance sheet form the information given would show the following:

				£
Capital employed				
Capital account balance as at 1 January 19X2				17,246
add Profit for the year				
deduct Drawings				3,120

	Cost	Depre-ciation	Net
	£	£	£
Represented by			
Fixed assets	20,000	10,000	10,000

	£	£	£
Current assets			
Stock		4,838	
Debtors		2,856	
Bank		2,221	
		9,915	
deduct Current liabilities			
Trade creditors	1,568		
Expense creditors	382	1,950	
Net current assets			7,965
			17,965

By using the formula

$$\text{Capital} = \text{Assets} - \text{Liabilities}$$

the total capital employed figure can be inserted and, by deduction, the profit figure for the year obtained.

It is, of course, possible to calculate the above profit by using the formula

$$\text{Profit} = (A - L)_2 - (A - L)_1 + \text{Drawings in the year}.$$

Confirm this for yourself.

Also note that the balance sheet is presented in a slightly different form to that used consistently in the text.

14.3S

Bobbin
Trading and Profit and Loss Account
for the year ended 31 March 19X7

	£	£
Sales		13,645
Cost of sales		
Opening stock	1,250	
Purchases	10,426	
	11,676	
less Closing stock	1,456	10,220
Gross profit		3,425
less Expenses		
Wages and National Insurance	597	
Rent	400	
Rates	196	
Electricity	66	
Shop expenses	104	
Depreciation of fixtures and fittings	60	1,423
Net profit		2,002

Balance Sheet as at 31 March 19X7

Assets

	Cost £	Depreciation £	Net £
Fixed assets			
Goodwill	2,000	–	2,000
Fixtures and fittings	600	60	540
	2,600	60	2,540
Current assets			
Stock at cost		1,456	
Cash at bank		3,655	
Cash in hand		112	
		5,223	
less Current liabilities			
Creditors		385	
Net current assets			4,838
			7,378
Financed by			
Capital account			
Amount introduced		6,000	
add Net profit for the year		2,002	
		8,002	
less Drawings		624	
			7,378

Tutorial notes

1. The amount of £3,750 paid to Reel Ltd is made up as follows:

	£
Fixtures and fittings	500
Goodwill	2,000
Stock	1,250
	3,750

The debit side of the transaction is shown in the three separate accounts; the credit entry is, of course, shown in the bank account.

2. Cash payments made out of takings, plus the balance of cash in hand, represents cash received for sales. The double entry for this transaction is – debit cash account, credit debtors.

3. Since there are neither opening debtors nor closing debtors in this question, sales for the year are simply the cash received, i.e. the figure which has been credited to debtors account.

4. Purchases for the year are calculated as follows:

	£
Cash paid during the year	
From bank account	10,000
From cash account	158
add Closing creditors	268
	10,426

5. Since Bobbin's lease is at £400 per annum, one quarter's rent has clearly not been paid at 31 March 19X7.

6. The figure of £385 shown in the balance sheet for creditors is made up as follows:

	£
Trade creditors	268
Electricity outstanding	17
Rent owing	100
	385

Workings

Bank account

19X6		£	19X6			£
Apr. 1 Capital		6,000	Apr. 1	Reel Ltd		3,750
Apr. 1				Fixtures		100
to			Apr. 1	Purchases for		
Mar. 31 Shop bankings		12,050	to	resale		10,000
			Mar. 31	Rent		300
				Rates		196
				Electricity		49
			Mar. 31	Balance c/d		3,655
		18,050				18,050
19X7						
Apr. 1 Balance b/d		3,655				

Capital account

			19X6		£
			Apr. 1 Bank		6,000

Debtors

19X7		£	19X7		£
Mar. 31 Sales		13,645	Mar. 31 Bank		12,050
			Cash		1,595
		13,645			13,645

Stock

19X6		£	
Apr. 1 Bank – Reel Ltd		1,250	

Fixtures and fittings

19X6		£	
Apr. 1 Bank – Reel Ltd		500	
Bank		100	

Goodwill

19X6		£	
Apr. 1 Bank – Reel Ltd		2,000	

Creditors

19X7		£	19X7		£
Mar. 31 Bank		10,000	Mar. 31 Purchases		10,426
Cash		158			
Balance c/d		268			
		10,426			10,426
			Apr. 1 Balance b/d		268

Rent

19X7		£	
Mar. 31 Bank		300	

Rates

19X7		£	
Mar. 31 Bank		196	

Electricity

19X7		£	
Mar. 31 Bank		49	

Cash

19X7		£	19X7		£
Mar. 31 Debtors		1,595	Mar. 31 Wages and National Insurance		597
			Purchases for resale		158
			Shop expenses		104
			Drawings		624
			Balance c/d		112
		1,595			1,595
Apr. 1 Balance b/d		112			

Wages and National Insurance

19X7	£		
Mar. 31 Cash	597		

Shop expenses

19X7	£		
Mar. 31 Cash	104		

Drawings

19X7	£		
Mar. 31 Cash	624		

Sales

		19X7	£
		Mar. 31 Debtors	13,645

Purchases

19X7	£		
Mar. 31 Creditors	10,426		

Bobbin
Trial Balance at 31 March 19X7

			Dr. £	Cr. £
Bank		B	3,655	
Capital		B		6,000
Stock		T	1,250	
Fixtures and fittings	A(4)	B	600	
Goodwill		B	2,000	
Creditors		B		268
Rent	A(3)	P	300	
Rates		P	196	
Electricity	A(2)	P	49	
Cash		B	112	
Wages and National Insurance		P	597	
Shop expenses		P	104	
Drawings		B	624	
Sales		T		13,645
Purchases		T	10,426	
			19,913	19,913

Accruals, prepayments, etc., at 31 March 19X7

1. Stock, at cost	£1,456	T and B
2. Electricity outstanding	£17	P and B
3. Rent owing	£100	P and B
4. Depreciate fixtures and fittings at a rate of 10% per annum		P and B

14.4S

I. Patchett
Profit and Loss Account for the period
1 July to 30 November 19X7

	£	£	£
Contract receipts			3,763
Materials consumed			
Opening stock		185	
Purchases		1,272	
		1,457	
less Closing stock		200	
		1,257	
Wages and National Insurance		748	
Rent		85	
Rates		35	
Electricity		38	
Van expenses		74	
Sundry expenses		49	
Depreciation – Motor van	50		
Plant and equipment	25	75	
			2,361
Net profit			1,402

Balance Sheet as at 30 November 19X7

	£	£
Assets		
Fixed assets at valuation		
Motor van		250
Plant and equipment		75
		325
Current assets		
Stock at valuation	200	
Debtors	204	
Cash at bank	3,757	
Cash in hand	12	
	4,173	
less Current liabilities		
Creditors	394	
Net current assets		3,779
		4,104

	£	£
Financed by		
Capital account		
Balance as at 30 June 19X7	2,654	
Amount introduced during the period	500	
	3,154	
add Net profit for the period	1,402	
	4,556	
less Drawings	452	4,104

Tutorial notes
1. The debit of £452 to drawings account from the cash account is the balancing figure.
2. You are required to prepare Patchett's *profit and loss account*, you are not asked to calculate a gross profit because obviously there is no such thing in a contractor's accounts.
3. Since Patchett was a contractor, his income would be receipts from contracts he carried out as opposed to 'sales' of some commodity or other. The calculation of contract receipts is made in the same way as the calculation of sales is made in a retail business, i.e. cash received + closing debtors − opening debtors.
4. In the capital account shown in the balance sheet, the amount introduced during the period is shown separately.
5. The fixed assets and stock are shown at valuation at the balance sheet date because the question states that this is to be done.
6. Debtors and creditors shown in the balance sheet are as follows:

Debtors		Creditors	
	£		£
Trade debtors	176	Trade creditors	349
Rates prepaid	28	Electricity owing	11
	—	Rent owing	34
	204		—
			394

Workings
Since the balance sheet as at 30 June 19X7 is given, there is no necessity to prepare an opening statement of affairs. The T accounts can be opened from the figures given in the balance sheet.

Capital		Creditors		Rates		Electricity	
£	£	£	£	£	£	£	£
	2,654	1,023	256	84	21	41	14
	500	156	1,272				
		349					
		1,528	1,528				
			349				

Motor van at cost				Depreciation on motor van	
£	£			£	£
450					150

Plant and equipment at cost				Depreciation on plant and equipment	
£	£			£	£
250					150

Stock		Debtors		Cash		Rent	
£	£	£	£	£	£	£	£
185		75	3,662	15	748	51	
		3,763	176	1,402	156		
					49		
		3,838	3,838		452		
					12		
		176		1,417	1,417		
				12			

Van expenses		Wages and National Insurance		Sundry expenses		Drawings	
£	£	£	£	£	£	£	£
74		748		49		452	

Contract receipts		Purchases	
£	£	£	£
	3,763	1,272	

The bank account has not been shown because it is analysed on the question paper.

Trial Balance as at 30 November 19X7

			Dr. £	Cr. £
Capital		B		3,154
Creditors		B		349
Rates	A(3)	P	63	
Electricity	A(2)	P	27	
Motor van at cost		B	450	
Depreciation on motor van	A(5)	B		150
Plant and equipment at cost		B	250	
Depreciation on plant and equipment	A(5)	B		150
Stock at 30 June 19X7		P	185	
Debtors		B	176	
Cash		B	12	
Bank		B	3,757	
Rent	A(4)	P	51	
Van expenses		P	74	

		£	£
Wages and National Insurance	P	748	
Sundry expenses	P	49	
Drawings	B	452	
Contract receipts	P		3,763
Purchases	P	1,272	
		7,566	7,566

Accruals, prepayments, etc.	£	
1. Stock at valuation	200	P and B
2. Electricity outstanding	11	P and B
3. Rates prepaid	28	P and B
4. Rent owing	34	P and B
5. Depreciation to be provided:		
Motor van	50	P and B
Plant and equipment	25	P and B

14.5S

Angus
Profit and Loss Account
for the year ended 31 March 19X6

	£	£	£
Sales			
Crops		4,568	
Livestock		996	
Milk		3,111	8,675
Subsidies and grants			
Crop deficiency payments		217	
Ploughing grant		145	362
			9,037
Livestock expenses			
Purchases	426		
Feeding stuffs	2,026		
Veterinary fees	55	2,507	
Crop expenses			
Seeds and fertilisers	728		
Threshing and baling	273	1,001	
Establishment expenses			
Rent and rates	483		
Electricity	77	560	
Administration and general expenses			
Wages and National Insurance	1,109		
Tractor and machinery repairs	537		
Tractor and machinery depreciation	425		
Sundry expenses	29	2,100	
		6,168	

	£	£	£
Stock valuation adjustment			
Opening valuation	2,025		
Closing valuation	1,940	85	6,253
Net profit			2,784

Balance Sheet as at 31 March 19X6

Assets	Cost	Depre-ciation	Net
	£	£	£
Fixed assets			
Tractor	700	100	600
Machinery	1,625	325	1,300
	2,325	425	1,900
Current assets			
Stocks, at valuation:			
Livestock	1,700		
Crops, produce and fertilisers	240	1,940	
Debtor		294	
Cash at bank		668	
		2,902	
less Current liabilities			
Creditor		21	
Net current assets			2,881
			4,781
Financed by			
Capital account			
Balance at 1 April 19X5		4,621	
add Net profit for year		2,784	
		7,405	
less Drawings		2,624	4,781

Tutorial notes
1. Although this question is for a specialist type of organisation, i.e. a farmer, the suggested method of dealing with incomplete record qustions can and should be applied.
2. Angus receives his farm income from sales under three different heads, i.e. crops, livestock and milk. This fact is clearly shown in the profit and loss account where the sales for the year have been analysed under the headings given. Since there are no debtors at

31 March 19X6 for either sales of crops or of livestock the amount received under each of those heads is obviously the sales figure for the year. On the other hand, since there are both opening and closing debtors relating to milk sales, the milk sales figure for the year must be calculated using the formula given in the text.

3. Subsidies and grants are clearly income but just as clearly they do not represent income from sales. A separate heading is thus shown in the profit and loss account.

4. The expenses for the year have been analysed and shown in generally accepted categories.

5. Since a tenant farmer does not 'trade', it is not possible to include the stocks in a trading account. Obviously stocks must be taken into account in calculating profit for the year. Note that if the closing valuation had exceeded the opening valuation, the adjustment would have been deducted from the total of the expenses.

Workings

Statement of Affairs at 31 March 19X5

	£
Tractor	360
Machinery	1,500
Stocks – Livestock	1,825
Crops, produce and fertilisers	200
Debtor – Milk Marketing Board	267
Bank	492
	4,644
Creditor – Electricity	23
Capital – balancing figure	4,621
	4,644

Bank		Milk Marketing Board		Electricity		Tractor	
£	£	£	£	£	£	£	£
492	340	267	294	79	23	360	360
3,084	728	3,111	3,084				
145	1,296					700	
217	537	3,378	3,378				
570	55			Machinery		Stocks	
1,724	125	294		£	£	£	£
	483			1,500		1,825	
	2,000			125		200	
	668						
6,232	6,232						
668							

Capital			Ploughing grant			Cereal deficiency payments	
£	£		£	£		£	£
	4,621			145			217

Cattle auctions			Crop sales			Seeds and fertilisers	
£	£		£	£		£	£
996	570		4,568	1,724		728	
	426			1,841			
—	—			273			
996	996			730			
			4,568	4,568			

Feedings stuffs			Tractor and machinery expenses			Veterinary fees	
£	£		£	£		£	£
1,296			537			55	
730							

Rent and rates			Drawings			Cash	
£	£		£	£		£	£
483			2,000			1,841	79
			624				1,109
							624
							29
						1,841	1,841

Wages and National Insurance			Sundry expenses			Threshing and baling	
£	£		£	£		£	£
1,109			29			273	

Sales			Cattle purchases	
£	£		£	£
	3,111		426	
	996			
	4,568			

The bank account has been included above in T account form for the convenience of students who wish to check the double entry of the transactions.

			Dr. £	Cr. £
Bank		B	668	
Milk Marketing Board		B	294	
Electricity	A(2)	P	56	
Tractor		B	700	
Machinery		B	1,625	
Stock at 31 March 19X5		P	2,025	
Capital		B		4,621
Ploughing grant		P		145
Cereal deficiency payments		P		217
Seeds and fertilisers		P	728	
Feeding stuffs		P	2,026	
Tractor and machinery expenses		P	537	
Veterinary fees		P	55	
Rent and rates		P	483	
Drawings		B	2,624	
Wages and National Insurance		P	1,109	
Sundry expenses		P	29	
Threshing and baling		P	273	
Sales – Crops		P		4,568
– Livestock		P		996
– Milk		P		3,111
Cattle purchases		P	426	
			13,658	13,658

Accruals, prepayments, etc.	£	
1. Stocks, at valuation	1,940	P and B
2. Electricity outstanding	21	P and B
3. Depreciation to be provided:		
Tractor	100	P and B
Machinery	325	P and B

15 Income and expenditure accounts

15.1S (a)

Darset Old Comrades Club
Cash summary for the year ended 31 December 19X8

	£	£
Receipts		
Bar takings		40,612
Subscriptions		3,050
Cash from bank		5,848
		49,510
Payments		
Bank deposits	42,610	
Petty cash and wages	4,435	47,045
Claimable from insurance company		2,465

(b)

Income and Expenditure Account
for the year ended 31 December 19X8

	£	£
Income		
Subscriptions		3,050
Profit on bar (Note 1)		4,854
		7,904
less Expenses		
Wages and National Insurance	2,868	
Rent and rates	499	
Insurance	39	
Light and heat	152	
Glasses, crockery and maintenance	1,310	
Telephone	59	
Sundry expenses	257	5,184
Surplus of income		2,720

Note
1. Bar profit and loss account

	£	£
Takings		40,612
Cost of sales		
Opening stock	3,607	
Purchases	35,067	
	38,674	
less Closing stock	2,916	35,758
Profit		4,854

Workings

Rent and rates

	£		£
Rates prepaid b/d	26	Rent owing b/d	41
Bank	460	Rates prepaid c/d	28
Rent owing c/d	82	Income and expenditure	499
	568		568
Rates prepaid b/d	28	Rent owing b/d	82

Light and heat

	£		£
Bank	156	Electricity owing b/d	22
Electricity owing c/d	18	Income and expenditure	152
	174		174
		Electricity owing b/d	18

15.2S (a)

Seaside Golf Club
Income and Expenditure Account
for the year ended 30 September 19X0

	£	£
Income		
Subscriptions		5,920
Entrance fees		580
Green fees		4,012
Profit on bar (Note 1)		6,772
		17,284
less Expenses		
Wages and National Insurance	5,585	
Professional's retainer	1,500	
Rent and rates	1,652	
Light and heat	367	
Telephone	154	

	£	£
Postages and stationery	182	
General expenses	362	
Fertilisers and seed	1,122	
Depreciation: Club house	600	
Fixtures and fittings	750	
Equipment	1,580	13,854

Excess of income over expenditure	3,430
add Profit on sale of mower	100
Surplus of income	3,530

Note
1. Bar profit and loss account

	£	£
Receipts		28,805
less Stock at 1 October 19X9	414	
Purchases	21,974	
	22,388	
deduct Stock at 30 September 19X0	355	
Cost of sales		22,033
		6,772

Balance Sheet as at 30 September 19X0

Assets	Valua-tion £	Depre-ciation £	Net £
Fixed assets			
Club house	30,000	600	29,400
Fixtures and fittings	7,500	750	6,750
Equipment	7,900	1,580	6,320
	45,400	2,930	42,470
Current assets			
Bar stock at cost		355	
Debtors		250	
Cash at bank		7,041	
Cash in hand		31	
		7,677	
Current liabilities			
less Creditors		550	
Net current assets			7,127
			49,597

	Valuation £	Depreciation £	Net £
Financed by			
Capital account			
Balance at 1 October 19X9			46,067
add Surplus for year			3,530
			49,597

(b) The receipts and payments account of the Seaside Golf Club would not be acceptable as an account of the transaction of the Club for the year, because of the following:
1. It does not show a true and complete picture of the income and expenses for the period, since (i) expenditure relating to periods other than the year to 30 September 19X0 is included, i.e. the accounts have not been prepared in accordance with the matching convention; (ii) capital expenditure is included in the account.
2. The assets and liabilities of the Seaside Golf Club as at 30 September 19X0 are not shown.

Tutorial notes
1. The subscription outstanding from one member for 19X8/19X9, £50, together with the 19X9/19X0 subscription for the same member, £55, have been written off.
2. Debtors

	£
Subscriptions due	70
Rates prepaid	180
	250

3. Creditors

	£
Rent owing	140
Bar purchases owing	410
	550

Workings
All workings are given in abbreviated form for this one solution.

Calculation of Capital Account at 1 October 19X9

	£	£
Cash at bank	2,548	
Cash in hand	65	
Subscriptions	150	
Rent		120
Rates	160	

	£	£
Bar purchases		250
Bar stock	414	
Club house	30,000	
Fixtures and fittings	7,500	
Equipment	5,600	
Capital account		46,067
	46,437	46,437

Subscriptions		Rent and rates		Bar purchases		Bar stock	
£	£	£	£	£	£	£	£
	150 6,000	160 1,652	120	21,814	250	414	

Club house		Fixtures and fittings		Equipment		Capital account	
£	£	£	£	£	£	£	£
30,000		7,500		5,600 2,200 300	200		46,067

Entrance fees		Green fees		Bar receipts		Telephone	
£	£	£	£	£	£	£	£
	580		4,012		28,805	154	

Light and heat		Postage and stationery		Wages and National Insurance		Professional's retainer	
£	£	£	£	£	£	£	£
367		182		5,585		1,500	

Fertilisers and seed		General expenses		Disposal of asset	
£	£	£	£	£	£
1,122		362		200	300

Trial Balance at 30 September 19X0

			£	£
Cash at bank		B	7,041	
Cash in hand		B	31	
Subscriptions		A(2) I		5,850
Rent and rates	A(3)	A(4) I	1,692	
Bar purchases		A(5) I	21,564	
Bar stock at 1 October 19X9		I	414	
Club house		A(6) B	30,000	
Fixtures and fittings		A(6) B	7,500	
Equipment		A(6) B	7,900	
Capital		B		46,067
Entrance fees		I		580
Green fees		I		4,012
Bar receipts		I		28,805

		£	£
Telephone	I	154	
Light and heat	I	367	
Postage and stationery	I	182	
Wages and National Insurance	I	5,585	
Professional's retainer	I	1,500	
Fertiliser's and seed	I	1,122	
General expenses	I	362	
Profit on disposal of equipment	I		100
		85,414	85,414

Accruals, prepayments, etc.	£	
1. Bar stock at 30 September 19X0	355	I and B
2. Subscriptions due	70	I and B
		(write off £105)
3. Rent owing	140	I and B
4. Rates prepaid	180	I and B
5. Bar purchases owing	410	I and B
6. Depreciation:		
Club house, 2% reducing balance		I and B
Fixtures and fittings, 10% reducing balance		I and B
Equipment, 20% reducing balance		I and B

15.3S (a)

Midon Cricket Club
Receipts and Expenditure Account
for the year ended 31 December 19X6

	£	£
Income		
Joining fees	56	
Subscriptions	412	468
Profit on bar (Note 1)		1,100
Surplus on cricket festival		196
Interest on investments		35
		1,799
less Expenses		
Wages and National Insurance	741	
Rent and rates	243	
Heating and lighting	108	
Postage and stationery	75	
General expenses	102	
Ground expenses	56	
Depreciation: Fixtures and fittings	63	
Machines	49	
Loss on sale of mowing machine	5	1,442
Surplus of income		357

(b)   *Balance Sheet as at 31 December 19X6*

Assets	Cost or valuation £	Depre- ciation £	Net £
Fixed assets			
Fixtures and fittings	504	63	441
Machines and equipment	270	48	222
	774	111	663

		£	
Investment – £1,000 7% Wessex Loan Stock			1,000
Current assets			
Bar stock		426	
Debtors (Note 2)		21	
Cash at bank		362	
Cash in hand		36	
		845	
less Current liabilities			
Creditors (Note 3)		47	
Net current assets			798
			2,461
Financed by			
Accumulated fund			
Balance at 1 December 19X6			2,104
add Surplus income for the year			357
			2,461

Notes to the accounts
1. Bar profit and loss account

	£	£
Bar sales		5,200
less Stock at 1 January 19X6	397	
Purchases	4,129	
	4,526	
deduct Stock at 31 December 19X6	426	4,100
Profit		1,100

2. Debtors

	£
Rates prepaid	21

113

3. Creditors

	£
Rent owing	35
Heating and lighting owing	12
	47

Workings

1. Accumulated fund at 1 January 19X6

	£	£
Fixtures and fittings at valuation		504
Machines and equipment at valuation		200
Bar stock		397
Rates prepaid		19
Cash at bank		997
Cash in hand		21
		2,138
less Rent accrued	20	
Heating and lighting accrued	14	34
		2,104

2. Rent and rates

	£	£
Rates prepaid at 1 January 19X6		19
Paid during year		230
Rent owing at 31 December 19X6		35
		284
less Rent owing at 1 January 19X6	20	
Rates prepaid 31 December 19X6	21	41
		243

3. Heating and lighting

	£
Paid during year	110
Owing at 31 December 19X6	12
	122
less Owing at 1 January 19X6	14
	108

4. Depreciation of machines (at 20% per annum)

	£
On (£200 − £20) for 12 months	36
On £90 for 8 months	12
On £20 for 4 months	1
	49

5. Loss on sale of mowing machine

	£	£
Valuation at 31 December 19X5		20
less Depreciation for 4 months	1	
Trade-in allowance	14	15
		5

15.4S (a)

Alway Social Club
Estimated bank account
for the year ending 31 March 19X6

	£		£
Balance at 1 April 19X5	980	Clubhouse extension	1,000
Subscriptions	1,506	New sports equipment	340
Sale of sports equipment	50	Bar purchases	11,800
Bar sales	14,875	Bar steward's wages	1,200
Admission charges for		Commission	149
socials	2,400	Expenses of socials	1,680
		Insurance	80
		Bar licence	50
		Rates	500
		Heat and light	250
		Miscellaneous	70
		Balance at 31 March	
		19X6 c/d	2,692
	19,811		19,811
Balance b/d	2,692		

(b)   *Estimated Bar Trading and Profit and Loss Account*
             for the year ending 31 March 19X6

	£	£
Sales		14,875
Cost of sales		
Opening stock	400	
Purchases	12,000	
	12,400	
less Closing stock	500	11,900
Gross profit		2,975
less Expenses		
Bar licence	50	
Wages	1,200	
Commission	149	1,399
Estimated profit		1,576

(c)   *Estimated Income and Expenditure Account*
             for the year ending 31 March 19X6

	£	£
Income		
Subscriptions		1,498
Profit on bar		1,576
Surplus on social evenings		720
		3,794
less Expenses		
Rates	475	
Heat and light	220	
Insurance	75	
Miscellaneous	70	
Depreciation of equipment	597	
Loss on sale of equipment	50	1,487
Estimated surplus of income		2,307

Estimated Balance Sheet as at 31 March 19X6

Assets	Cost	Depre-ciation	Net
	£	£	£
Fixed assets			
Clubhouse	9,900	–	9,900
Equipment	2,390	1,547	843
	12,290	1,547	10,743

Current assets		
Stock	500	
Debtors (Note 1)	165	
Cash at bank	2,692	
Cash in hand	10	
	3,367	
less Current liabilities		
Creditors (Note 2)	1,500	
Net current assets		1,867
		12,610

Financed by	
Accumulated fund	
Balance at 1 April 19X5	10,303
add Surplus income for the year	2,307
	12,610

Notes to balance sheet
1. Debtors

	£
Rates prepaid	125
Insurance prepaid	40
	165

2. Creditors

	£
Creditors for bar purchases	1,000
Clubhouse extension	500
	1,500

Workings
1. Accumulated fund at 1 April 19X5

Fixed assets	Cost	Depre-ciation	Net
	£	£	£
Clubhouse	8,400	–	8,400
Equipment	2,300	1,100	1,200
	10,700	1,100	9,600

Current assets		
Stocks		400
Debtors		151
Cash at bank		980
Cash in hand		10
		1,541
less Current liabilities		
Creditors		838
Net current assets		703
Accumulated fund		10,303

Debtors	£	Creditors	£
Rates prepaid	100	Creditors for bar purchases	800
Insurance prepaid	35	Subscriptions in advance	8
Subscriptions in arrears	16	Electricity owing	30
	151		838

2. Subscriptions – cash received

	£
In arrears	16
Current – 298 members at £5 per annum	1,490
	1,506

3. Bar purchases

	£
Bar stocks at 31 March 19X5	400
Increase in costs from 1 April 19X5 – 25%	100
Equivalent to one-half of one month's purchases	500
Purchases for 12 months – 24 × £500	£12,000

4. Payments for bar purchases

	£
Outstanding at 31 March 19X5	800
Purchases for 11 months	11,000
	11,800

5. Bar sales

	£
Cost of sales per bar trading account	11,900
Gross profit at 20% on sales	2,975
	14,875

6. Equipment

	Cost	Depre- ciation
	£	£
Balances at 31 March 19X5	2,300	1,100
less Sold during year	250	150
	2,050	950
add New equipment	340	
At 31 March 19X6	2,390	
Depreciation at 25%		597
At 31 March 19X6		1,547

7. Clubhouse

	£
Cost	8,400
Extensions	1,500
	9,900

16 Limited companies

16.1S (a)

Blackbird Ltd
Trading, Profit and Loss and Appropriation Account
for the year to 31 May 19X1

	£	£
Sales		800,000
Cost of sales		
Stock at 1 June 19X0	142,480	
Purchases	438,560	
	581,040	
less Stock at 31 May 19X1	155,460	425,580
Gross profit		374,420
add Provision for doubtful debts no longer required		2,000
Discount received		17,640
		394,060
less Administration expenses (Note 1)	79,900	
Selling and distribution expenses (Note 2)	55,760	
Depreciation – on buildings	43,000	
– on furniture and fittings	7,500	
Debenture interest	9,000	195,160
Net profit		198,900
Transfer to general reserve	100,000	
Dividend paid		
Interim preference of 5%	10,000	
Dividends proposed		
Final preference of 5%	10,000	
Ordinary of 15%	30,000	150,000
		48,900
Undistributed profit at 1 June 19X0		20,560
Undistributed profit carried forward		69,460

Balance Sheet as at 31 May 19X1

Assets	Cost	Depre-ciation	Net
	£	£	£
Fixed assets			
Land	230,000	–	230,000
Buildings	430,000	103,000	327,000
Furniture and fittings	80,000	37,500	42,500
	740,000	140,500	599,500
Goodwill at cost			164,000
Current assets			
Stock at cost		155,460	
Debtors (Note 3)		122,120	
Cash in hand		880	
		278,460	
less Current liabilities			
Creditors (Note 4)	73,000		
Bank overdraft	59,500		
Proposed dividends	40,000	172,500	
Net current assets			105,960
			869,460
Financed by			
Share capital – authorised and issued			
10% £1 preference shares		200,000	
£1 ordinary shares		200,000	400,000
Reserves			
Share premium		100,000	
General reserve		200,000	
Profit and loss account		69,460	369,460
Shareholders' funds			769,460
Loan capital			
9% debentures			100,000
			869,460

(b) (i) A share premium is the difference between the issue price of shares and their par value. In relation to the accounts of Black-bird Ltd, the share premium account would have arisen when some of the shares were issued at a price above £1 each.

(ii) Non-distributable reserves – Share premium
Distributable reserves – General reserve
Profit and loss account

Non-distributable reserves usually have some legal restriction placed on their use and are not available for the purposes of dividend distribution. Distributable reserves are all available for distribution to shareholders assuming the cash is available.

Notes

1. Administration expenses

	£
Per trial balance	81,620
less Paid in advance	1,720
	79,900

2. Selling and distribution expenses

	£
Per trial balance	50,260
add Amounts owing	5,500
	55,760

3. Debtors

	£
Per trial balance	126,400
Administration expenses paid in advance	1,720
	128,120
less Provision for doubtful debts	6,000
	122,120

4. Creditors

	£
Per trial balance	63,000
Selling and distribution expenses owing	5,500
Debenture interest owing	4,500
	73,000

16.2S

VHR Limited
Operating Statement for the year ended 31 December 19X6

		£	£	£
Sales				400,000
Cost of sales				
(a)	Raw materials consumed (Note 1)	150,000		
	Manufacturing wages	60,000		
(b) Prime cost		210,000		
	Manufacturing overhead expenses (Note 2)	89,200		

	£	£	£
Manufacturing cost		299,200	
add Work in progress, 1 January 19X6		16,000	
		315,200	
less Work in progress,			
31 December 19X6		18,200	
(c) Cost of finished goods produced		297,000	
Finished goods stock at			
1 January 19X6	51,000		
Purchases	9,000		
	60,000		
less Finished goods stock at			
31 December 19X6	57,000	3,000	
(d) Cost of finished goods sold			300,000
(e) Gross profit			100,000
Administration expenses (Note 3)		22,000	
Selling and distribution			
expenses (Note 4)		41,000	63,000
(f) Net profit before taxation			37,000

Notes

1. Raw materials consumed

	£
Stock at 1 January 19X6	39,000
Purchases	152,000
	191,000
less Stock at 31 December 19X6	41,000
	150,000

2. Manufacturing overhead expenses

	£
Manufacturing expenses	25,300
Repairs and maintenance of plant and machinery	13,500
Depreciation of factory	38,000
Power	10,000
Light and heat: factory	2,400
	89,200

3. Administration expenses

	£
Light and heat: general office	800
Depreciation of general offices	5,000
Miscellaneous	16,200
	22,000

4. Selling and distribution expenses

	£
Light and heat: sales warehouse and offices	1,300
Depreciation of sales warehouse and offices	7,000
Carriage outwards	6,600
Miscellaneous	26,100
	41,000

16.3S (a)

D. Yorke Ltd
Profit and Loss Appropriation Account
for the period ended 30 June 19X5

	£	£
Net profit for the period (Note 1)		12,670
Undistributed profit at 1 July 19X4		12,126
Profit available for distribution		24,796
Transfer to general reserve	6,000	
Dividends proposed		
Preference of 8%	1,600	
Ordinary of 10%	6,000	13,600
Undistributed profit carried forward		11,196

Tutorial note

Many accountants, including the authors, prefer the undistributed profit brought forward to be shown in the appropriation account after the appropriations for the year have been made. In this question, however, the appropriations made exceeded the net profit for the period ended 30 June 19X5. To avoid showing a debit balance on the profit and loss account, albeit a temporary one, the undistributed profit brought forward at 1 July 19X4 was added to the net profit for the period before the appropriations were made.

There is no legal reason to prevent the undistributed profits being shown as above; it is simply a matter of preference.

Balance Sheet as at 30 June 19X5

Assets	Cost	Depre- ciation	Net
	£	£	£
Fixed assets			
Land and buildings	66,100	–	66,100
Office fittings and equipment	22,320	11,948	10,372
Vehicles	9,700	8,240	1,460
	98,120	20,188	77,932

	Cost £	Depreciation £	Net £
Current assets			
Stock		41,926	
Debtors (Note 2)		13,675	
Cash at bank		3,898	
		59,499	
less Current liabilities			
Creditors (Note 3)	10,635		
Proposed dividends	7,600	18,235	
Net current assets			41,264
			119,196
Financed by			
Share capital – authorised and issued			
8% £1 preference shares		20,000	
£1 ordinary shares		60,000	80,000
Reserves			
General reserve		20,000	
Profit and loss account		11,196	31,196
Shareholders' funds			111,196
Loan capital			
10% debentures			8,000
			119,196

(b) Directors' fees are treated as an expense when measuring profit because the directors, as directors, are employees of the company. They may also be part owners of the company as shareholders, but the fees they receive are for their work in the capacity of employees.

In a partnership business, all the profit belongs to the partners who between them own the whole of the business. The way in which the profit is appropriated between the partners is for the partners themselves to decide and partnership salaries are simply part of that appropriation.

Notes
1. Net profit for the period

	£	£
Gross profit for the period		40,754
less Expenses:		
Wages and salaries	14,100	
Directors' fees (£1,250 + £2,500)	3,750	
Rates and insurances (£705 − £75)	630	
Light and heat (£608 + £274)	882	

	£	£
Postage and telephone	310	
General expenses	1,554	
Depreciation – office fittings and equipment	3,348	
– vehicles	1,940	
Debenture interest	800	
Audit fee	600	
Bad debts	170	28,084
		12,670

2. Debtors

	£
Per question	13,600
Insurance prepaid	75
	13,675

3. Creditors

	£
Per question	6,861
Electricity owing	274
Directors' fees	2,500
Audit fee	600
Debenture interest	400
	10,635

16.4S (a)

Skyblue Ltd
Trading and Profit and Loss Account
for the year ended 31 October 19X0

	£	£
Sales (Note 1)		1,821,000
Cost of goods sold		1,210,000
Gross profit		611,000
Discounts received		8,500
		619,500
less Expenses		
Wages and salaries	340,000	
Directors' emoluments (Note 2)	45,000	
Repairs and renewals (Note 3)	44,000	
Advertising (Note 4)	32,000	
Debenture interest (Note 5)	6,400	
Bank overdraft interest	4,300	
Discounts allowed	1,700	
Depreciation – of freehold property	14,000	
of fixtures and fittings	38,600	
Loss on sale of fixtures and fittings (Note 6)	15,000	541,000

	£	£
Net profit		78,500
Dividend paid – interim of 5%	20,000	
Dividend proposed – final of 2½%	10,000	30,000
		48,500
Undistributed profit at 31 October 19X9		158,300
Undistributed profit carried forward		206,800

Balance Sheet as at 31 October 19X0

Assets	Cost	Depreciation	Net
	£	£	£
Fixed assets			
Freehold property	280,000	105,000	175,000
Fixtures and fittings (Note 7)	386,000	179,600	206,400
	666,000	284,600	381,400
Current assets			
Stock at cost		230,000	
Deferred revenue expenditure			
(Note 4)		60,000	
Debtors (Note 8)		173,000	
Cash at bank		3,600	
		466,600	
less Current liabilities			
Creditors (Note 9)	32,200		
Bank overdraft	89,000		
Proposed dividend	10,000	131,200	
Net current assets			335,400
			716,800
Financed by			
Share capital			
£1 ordinary shares fully paid			400,000
Reserves			
Share premium		30,000	
Profit and loss account		206,800	236,800
Shareholders' funds			636,800
Loan capital			
8% debentures 19X9–19X0			80,000
			716,800

(b) Working capital is the excess of current assets over current liabilities – another name for net current assets. The importance of working capital lies in the ability of a business to pay for labour and goods and services as and when required and to take the benefit of available cash discounts. To be able to achieve these objectives will usually necessitate an adequate amount of cash within the current assets. But in considering working capital, attention must be given to the nature of the business as well as to the nature of the current assets and current liabilities.

Inadequate working capital is often the cause of business failures but businesses in different industries will have different working capital structures.

Notes
1. Sales

	£
Per trial balance	1,830,000
less Receipt from K. Bone wrongly credited	9,000
	1,821,000

2. Directors' emoluments

	£
Per trial balance	41,000
Amount accrued	4,000
	45,000

3. Repairs and renewals

	£
Per trial balance	60,000
less New fixtures and fittings	16,000
	44,000

4. Advertising

	£
Per trial balance	92,000
less Deferred revenue expenditure	60,000
	32,000

The deduction of deferred revenue expenditure will, of course, be in agreement with the 'matching concept'.

5. Debenture interest

	£
Per trial balance	3,200
Amount accrued	3,200
	6,400

6. Loss on sale of fixtures and fittings

	£	£
Cost		40,000
deduct Depreciation 10% × £40,000 × 3 years	12,000	
Sale proceeds	13,000	25,000
		15,000

7. Fixtures and fittings

	Cost £	Depreciation £
Per trial balance	410,000	153,000
Additions during year	16,000	
	426,000	
Sales during year	40,000	12,000
	386,000	141,000
Depreciation for the year		38,600
		179,600

8. Debtors

	£
Per trial balance	182,000
less Receipt from K. Bone	9,000
	173,000

9. Creditors

	£
Per trial balance	38,000
Directors' emoluments owing	4,000
Debenture interest owing	3,200
	45,200
less Receipt from sale of fixtures and fittings	13,000
	32,200

16.5S (a)

Greater Bargains Limited
Trading and Profit and Loss Account
for the year ended 31 March 19X0

	£	£
Sales		500,000
less Cost of sales		350,000
Gross profit		150,000
less Expenses		
Salaries	21,000	
Directors' emoluments	12,000	
Rates, light and heat (Note 1)	9,100	
Telephone and postages (Note 2)	6,500	
Motor vehicle expenses (Note 3)	25,900	
Depreciation – of fixtures and fittings	6,000	
– of motor vehicles	14,400	
Loss on sale of motor vehicle	1,700	96,600
Net profit		53,400
Dividend proposed		
Ordinary of 15%		30,000
		23,400
Undistributed profits at 31 March 19X9		15,000
Undistributed profits carried forward		38,400

Balance Sheet as at 31 March 19X0

Assets	Cost/ valuation £	Depre- ciation £	Net £
Fixed assets			
Freehold property (Note 4)	190,000	–	190,000
Fixtures and fittings	120,000	78,000	42,000
Motor vehicles	72,000	25,600	46,400
	382,000	103,600	278,400
Current assets			
Stock in trade, at cost		38,000	
Debtors (Note 5)		24,000	
Cash at bank		7,000	
		69,000	
less Current liabilities			
Creditors (Note 6)	9,000		
Proposed dividend	30,000	39,000	
Net current assets			30,000
			308,400

Financed by
Share capital

	Authorised	Issued and fully paid
	£	£
Ordinary shares of £1 each	250,000	200,000

Reserves

Share premium	20,000	
Revaluation reserve (Note 4)	50,000	
Profit and loss account	38,400	108,400
Shareholders' funds		308,400

(b) The functions of the profit and loss appropriation account in limited company accounts is to show the following: (1) the total net profit for an accounting period; (2) the amounts 'appropriated' for taxation, transfers to reserves and payment of dividends; (3) the undistributed profits carried forward.

Notes
1. Rates, light and heat

	£
Per list of balances	11,400
less Prepayment	2,300
	9,100

2. Telephone and postages

	£
Per list of balances	5,600
add Accrued charges	900
	6,500

3. Motor vehicle expenses

	£
Per list of balances	24,100
add Accrued charges	300
Sale of proceeds of vehicle credited in error	1,500
	25,900

4. Revaluation reserve

	£
Freehold property valuation	190,000
less Cost	140,000
	50,000

5. Debtors

	£
Per list of balances	21,700
Rates, light and heat prepaid	2,300
	24,000

6. Creditors

	£
Per list of balances	7,800
Accrued charges	
Telephone and postages	900
Motor vehicle expenses	300
	9,000

17 Taxation in company accounts

17.1S

Eureka Limited
Franked Investment Income

19XX		£	19XX		£
Dec. 31 Profit and Loss		24,000	Mar. 31 Bank		1,300
				Tax attributable to F.I.I.	700
			Jun. 30 Bank		3,900
				Tax attributable to F.I.I.	2,100
			Sep. 30 Bank		10,400
				Tax attributable to F.I.I.	5,600
		24,000			24,000

Tax attributable to Franked Investment Income

19XX	£	19XX	£
Mar. 31 Franked investment income	700	Dec. 31 Profit and Loss (taxation charge)	8,400
Jan. 30 Franked investment income	2,100		
Sep. 30 Franked invesment income	5,600		
	8,400		8,400

Franked Payments

19XX	£	19XX	£
Jan. 30 Bank	13,000	Dec. 31 Profit and Loss	130,000
Dec. 31 Bank	117,000		
	130,000		130,000

Advanced Corporation Tax

19XX		£	19XX	£
Jul. 14 Bank		4,200	Dec. 31 Corporation Tax	61,600
Dec. 31 Balance	c/d	57,400		
		61,600		61,600
			19XX	
			Jan. 1 Balance	b/d 57,400

133

Notes for students

1. The advance corporation tax paid on 14 July is calculated as follows:

	£	£
Jun. 30 Franked payment	13,000	
Act 35/65	7,000	20,000
Less Franked investment income to 30 June, including tax credit		8,000
		12,000

ACT paid £12,000 × 35%   =   £4,200

2. The advance corporation tax payable at 31 December is calculated as follows:

	£	£
Dec. 31 Franked payment	117,000	
ACT 35/65	63,000	180,000
Less Franked investment income to 30 September, including tax credit		16,000
		164,000

ACT payable £164,000 × 35%   =   57,400

17.2S

Humpledink Ltd
Corporation tax

19X5	£	19X5	£
Jan. 1 Advance corporation tax account	16,071	Jan. 1 Balances brought down Year end 31 December 19X3	52,000
1 Bank	35,929	Year end 31 December 19X4	60,000
Dec. 31 Profit and loss account Overprovision at year end 31 December 19X4	2,500	Dec. 31 Profit and loss account Year end 31 December 19X5	75,000
Dec. 31 Balances carried down Year end 31 December 19X4	57,500		
Year end 31 December 19X5	75,000		
	187,000		187,000
		19X6	
		Jan. 1 Balances brought down Year end 31 December 19X4	57,500
		Year end 31 December 19X5	75,000

Advance corporation tax

19X5		£	19X5		£
Jan. 1	Balances brought down		Jan. 1	Corporation tax	
	Year end 31			account	16,071
	December 19X3	16,071	Dec. 31	Deferred taxation	
	Year end 31			account	13,462
	December 19X4	18,470	Dec. 31	Balances carried down	
Jul. 14	Bank	6,731		Year end 31	
Dec. 31	Balance carried down			December 19X4	18,470
	ACT on proposed			Year end 31	
	dividend	13,462		December 19X5	6,731
		54,734			54,734
19X6			19X6		
Jan. 1	Balances brought down		Jan. 1	Balance brought down	
	Year end 31			ACT on proposed	
	December 19X4	18,470		dividend	13,462
	Year end 31				
	December 19X5	6,731			

Deferred taxation

19X5		£	19X5		£
Dec. 31	Advance corporation		Jan. 1	Balance b/d	26,500
	tax	13,462	Dec. 31	Profit and loss	
Dec. 31	Balance c/d	17,538		account	4,500
		31,000			31,000
			19X6		
			Jan. 1	Balance b/d	17,538

(b)
Profit and Loss Account
for the year ended 31 December 19X5

	£	£
Profit before taxation		150,000
Taxation on profit for the year		
Corporation tax at %	79,500	
less Corporation tax for previous year no		
longer required	2,500	77,000
Profit for the year after taxation		73,000
Dividend paid		
Interim dividend at 5p per share	12,500	
Dividend proposed		
Final dividend at 10p per share	25,000	37,500
Unappropriated profit for the year		35,500
Unappropriated profit brought forward		120,000
Unappropriated profit carried forward		155,500

(c)   *Balance Sheet as at 31 December 19X5*

	£	£
Current liabilities		
Corporation tax payable 1 January 19X6	39,030	
Advance corporation tax	13,462	52,492
Deferred liabilities		
Deferred taxation	17,538	
Corporation tax payable 1 January 19X7	68,269	85,807

Tutorial notes

1. The debit balances brought down on the ACT account would be transferred to the Corporation Tax account as and when the mainstream corporation tax was paid.
2. ACT on proposed dividend is debited to deferred taxation account and credited to advance corporation tax account. Since the ACT will be payable within twelve months of the balance sheet date, it is shown as a current liability in the balance sheet.
3. The double entry for the increase in corporation tax based on the accounting profit as opposed to the profit for taxation is

Profit and loss account	Debit
Deferred taxation account	Credit

VBA Limited
Manufacturing, Trading and Profit and Loss Account
for the year ended 31 December 19X7

	£000	£000
Sales		3,400
Cost of sales		
Materials consumed (Note 1)	1,030	
Manufacturing wages (Note 2)	360	
Prime cost	1,390	
Manufacturing expenses (Note 3)	720	
Manufacturing cost	2,110	
Work in progress at 1 January 19X7	40	
	2,150	
less Work in progress at 31 December 19X7	30	
Cost of finished goods produced	2,120	
Finished goods stock at 1 January 19X7	230	
	2,350	
less Finished goods stock at 31 December 19X7	300	2,050
Gross profit		1,350
Administration expenses (Note 4)	315	
Selling and distribution expenses (Note 5)	690	
Debenture interest	10	1,015
Trading profit		335
Profit on sale of fixed assets (Note 6)		5
Net profit before taxation		340
Taxation on profits for the year		170
Net profit for the year after taxation		170
Dividends paid – interim of 5%	50	
Dividends proposed – final of 10%	100	150
Unappropriated profit for the year		20
Unappropriated profit brought forward		580
Unappropriated profit carried forward		600

Balance Sheet as at 31 December 19X7

Assets

	Cost	Depreciation	Net
	£000	£000	£000
Fixed assets (Note 7)	1,990	790	1,200

Current assets			
Stocks (Note 8)		580	
Debtors (Note 9)		400	
Cash at bank and in hand		20	
		1,000	
less Current liabilities			
Creditors (Note 10)	112		
Taxation (Note 11)	118		
Proposed dividends	100	330	
Net current assets			670
			1,870

Financed by		
Share capital		
£1 ordinary shares		1,000
Reserves		
Profit and loss account		600
Shareholders' funds		1,600
Loan capital		
10% debentures		100
Taxation (Note 11)		170
		1,870

Notes

1. Materials consumed

	£000
Stock at 1 January 19X7	220
Purchases	1,060
	1,280
less Stock at 31 December 19X7	250
	1,030

2. Manufacturing wages

	£000
Per trial balance	353
Wages accrued	7
	360

3. Manufacturing expenses

	£000
Per trial balance	555
Accrued	6
Depreciation (see below)	160
	721
less Prepaid	1
	720

4. Administration expenses

	£000
Per trial balance	292
Accrued	5
Depreciation (see below)	20
	317
less Prepaid	2
	315

5. Selling and distribution expenses

	£000
Per trial balance	666
Accrued	1
Depreciation (see below)	20
Bad debts written off	3
Increase in provision for doubtful debts	1
	691
less Prepaid	1
	690

6. Profit on sale of fixed assets

	£000
Sale proceeds	15
less Net book value	10
	£5

7. Fixed assets

	£000
Per trial balance	2,090
less Cost of assets sold	100
	1,990

8. Stocks

	£000
Stock of materials	250
Work in progress	30
Stock of finished goods	300
	580

9. Debtors

		£000
Per trial balance		420
Prepayments		4
		424
less Bad debts	3	
Provision for doubtful debts	21	24
		400

10. Creditors

	£000
Per trial balance	88
Accruals	19
Debenture interest owing	5
	112

11. Taxation

	£
Taxation on 19X6 profits, payable 1 January 19X8	118
Taxation on 19X7 profits, payable 1 January 19X9	170

(Assuming the company began trading before 6 April 1965.)

Calculation of depreciation

	£000		£000
Cost of fixed assets per trial balance	2,090	10% for 9 months	12
less Purchased on 31 March 19X7	(160)	10% for 6 months	5
Sold on 30 June 19X7	(100)	10% for 12 months	183
Charge for the year	1,830		200

Allocation of depreciation

	£000
Manufacturing expense 80%	160
Administration expense 10%	20
Selling and distribution expense 10%	20
	200

CDM Limited

17.4S (a)   *Trading, Profit and Loss and Appropriation Accounts
for the year ended 31 March 19X7*

	Note	£	£
Sales	2		160,000
Cost of sales	1		120,000
Gross profit			40,000
add Discount received			2,900
Decrease in provision for bad debts			200
			43,100
less Expenses			
Business expenses	3	12,900	
Discounts allowed		3,800	
Bad debts		1,700	
Depreciation		8,700	27,100
Net profit before taxation			16,000
Taxation on profits for the year		8,100	
less Taxation for previous year no longer required	4	100	8,000
Net profit for the year after taxation			8,000
Unappropriated profit, brought forward			9,000
			17,000
Dividends – paid		7,500	
proposed		3,000	10,500
Unappropriated profit, carried forward			6,500

Balance Sheets as at 31 March

	Note	19X6 £	19X6 £	19X7 £	19X7 £
Assets					
Fixed assets:					
Cost		80,000		90,000	
less Depreciation		30,800		39,500	
			49,200		50,500
Current assets					
Stocks		28,000		29,000	
Debtors	5	22,800		19,000	
Cash at bank		8,000		7,100	
		58,800		55,100	
less Current liabilities					
Creditors		17,000		18,000	
Taxation		5,000		8,100	
Proposed dividends		7,000		3,000	
		29,000		29,100	
Net current assets			29,800		26,000
			79,000		76,500
Financed by					
Share capital					
Ordinary shares			70,000		70,000
Reserves					
Profit and loss					
account			9,000		6,500
			79,000		76,500

Notes

1. Cost of sales

	£	£
Opening stock		28,000
Purchases – Payments to creditors	117,100	
Discounts received	2,900	
Creditors at 31 March 19X7	18,000	
	138,000	
less Creditors at 31 March 19X6	17,000	121,000
		149,000
less Closing stock		29,000
		120,000

2. Sales

		£
Cost of sales		120,000
Add 33⅓ %		40,000
		160,000

3. Business expenses

	£	£	£
Opening cash balance			8,000
Cash received from debtors			
Sales		160,000	
Debtors at 31 March 19X6		24,000	
		184,000	
less Discounts allowed	3,800		
Bad debts written off	1,700		
Debtors at 31 March 19X7	20,000	25,500	158,500
			166,500
less Payments during year			
Creditors		117,100	
Fixed assets		10,000	
Taxation		4,900	
Dividends		14,500	146,500
			20,000
Closing cash balance			7,100
Expenses paid			12,900

4. Taxation for previous year no longer required

	£
Creditor for taxation at 31 March 19X6	5,000
Paid during the year	4,900
	100

5. Debtors

	31 March 19X6	31 March 19X7
	£	£
Per list of balances	24,000	20,000
less Provision for bad debts	1,200	1,000
	22,800	19,000

18

The issue and forfeiture of shares

18.1S

B. Booth Ltd
Journal

19XX		£	£
May 13 Bank		212,000	
	Application and allotment account		212,000
	Amount received on applications for 424,000 shares of £1 each – £0.50 per share.		
May 31	Application and allotment account	300,000	
	Share capital account		225,000
	Share premium account		75,000
	Amounts due on application and allotment of 300,000 shares of £1 each including a premium of £0.25 per share.		
	Application and allotment account	12,000	
	Bank account		12,000
	Money received on application refunded to unsuccessful applicants.		
Jun. 3	Bank account	100,000	
	Application and allotment account		100,000
	Money received on allotment of 300,000 shares of £1 each.		
Jul. 31	Call account	75,000	
	Share capital account		75,000
	Amount due on call of £0.25 per share on 300,000 shares of £1 each.		
Aug. 3	Bank	75,000	
	Call account		75,000
	Money received on call of £0.25 per share on 300,000 shares of £1 each.		

Cash book
Bank account

19XX		£	19XX		£
May 13	Application and allotment	212,000	May 31	Application and allotment	12,000
Jun. 3	Application and allotment	100,000	Aug. 3	Balance c/d	375,000
Aug. 3	Call account	75,000			
		387,000			387,000
Aug. 4	Balance b/d	375,000			

Tutorial note

Where the question asks for the entries on an issue of shares to be shown in the company's journal, it is usual to show all the entries, including those relating to cash, in the journal.

18.2S (a)

K. Boydell Ltd
Journal

19XX		£	£
Ordinary share capital account		1,200	
Forfeited shares account			1,200
Shares in the name of ———————, forfeited in accordance with resolution no. ————— , dated ——————— .			
Forfeited shares account		600	
First call account			300
Second call account			300
Transfer to forfeited shares account of the instalments unpaid on the ordinary shares in the name of ———————, now forfeited.			

(b)

	£	£
Share capital		
Authorised:		
200,000 ordinary shares of £1 each	200,000	
Issued:		
100,000 ordinary shares of £1 each, fully called		100,000
less Forfeited shares		1,200
		98,800
Reserves		
Forfeited shares account		600

18.3S

Grobigg Ltd
Application and allotment

19X8		£	19X8		£
Apr. 30	Bank – cash returned to unsuccessful applicants	6,000	Apr. 1	Bank – cash received on applications	135,000
	Ordinary share capital	120,000	May 3	Bank – cash received on allotment	13,500
	Share premium	22,500			
		148,500			148,500

Bank account

19X8		£	19X8		£
Apr. 1	Application and allotment	135,000	Apr. 30	Application and allotment	6,000
May 3	Application and allotment	13,500	Sep. 3	Balance c/d	172,780
Jun. 3	Call	29,920			
Sep. 3	Forfeited shares	360			
		178,780			178,780
Sep. 4	Balance b/d	172,780			

Ordinary share capital

19X8		£	19X8		£
Jul. 31	Forfeited shares	400	Apr. 30	Application and allotment	120,000
Sep. 3	Balance c/d	150,000	May 31	Call account	30,000
			Sep. 3	Forfeited shares	400
		150,400			150,400
			Sep. 4	Balance b/d	150,000

Share premium

19X8		£	19X8		£
Sep. 3	Balance c/d	22,780	Apr. 30	Application and allotment	22,500
			Sep. 3	Forfeited shares	280
		22,780			22,780
			Sep. 4	Balance b/d	22,780

Call account

19X8		£	19X8		£
May 31	Ordinary share capital	30,000	Jun. 3	Bank	29,920
			Jul. 31	Forfeited shares	80
		30,000			30,000

Forfeited shares

19X8		£	19X8		£
Jul. 31	Call	80	Jul. 31	Ordinary share capital	400
Sep. 3	Ordinary share capital	400	Sep. 3	Bank	360
Sep. 3	Share premium	280			
		760			760

146

19

Redemption of shares and the purchase by a company of its own shares

19.1S (a)

F. Davies Ltd
Redeemable preference share capital

19X3		£	19X3		£
Jul. 1	Preference share redemption	50,000	Jul. 1	Balance b/d	50,000

Premium on redemption of preference shares

19X3		£	19X3		£
Jul. 1	Preference share redemption	5,000	Jul. 1	Profit and loss	5,000

Profit and loss account

19X3		£	19X3		£
Jul. 1	Premium on redemption of preference shares	5,000	Jul. 1	Balance b/d	60,000
	Capital redemption reserve	50,000			
	Balance c/d	5,000			
		60,000			60,000
			Jul. 1	Balance b/d	5,000

Capital redemption reserve

			19X3		£
			Jul. 1	Profit and loss	50,000

Preference share redemption

19X3	£	19X3		£
Jul. 1 Bank	55,000	Jul. 1 Redeemable prefer- ence share capital	50,000	
		Premium on redemption of preference shares	5,000	
	55,000			55,000

Bank

19X3	£	19X3	£
Jul. 1 Balance b/d	85,000	Jul. 1 Preference share redemption	55,000
		Balance c/d	30,000
	85,000		85,000
Jul. 1 Balance b/d	30,000		

(b)   *Balance Sheet as at 1 July 19X3*

	£	£
Assets		
Fixed assets		105,000
Current assets (excluding cash)	95,000	
Cash at bank	30,000	
	125,000	
less Current liabilities	75,000	
Net current assets		50,000
		155,000
Financed by		
Share capital – authorised and issued		
Ordinary shares of £1 each		100,000
Reserves		
Capital redemption reserve		50,000
Profit and loss account		5,000
		155,000

19.2S (a) Where shares are redeemed out of accumulated profits, it is necessary to transfer to a capital redemption reserve an amount equal to the nominal value of the shares so redeemed. Since a capital redemption reserve may only be used in paying up unissued shares to be allotted as fully paid bonus shares, the creation of such a reserve has the effect of preserving the interests of creditors.

148

(b) Where shares are redeemed out of the proceeds of a new issue of shares, the new shares take the place of the redeemed shares in the share capital structure and creditors' interests are protected in this way. In such a case, therefore, it is not necessary to create a capital redemption reserve.

19.3S   *Traders Ltd*
                                             Journal

19X3		£	£
May 31 Bank		18,000	
	Investments		14,000
	Profit and loss		4,000
	Sale of investments and transfer of profit on sale.		
	Bank	25,000	
	Application and allotment		25,000
	Amount received on application for 20,000 ordinary shares of £1 each issued to shareholders at £1.25 each.		
	Application and allotment	25,000	
	Ordinary share capital		20,000
	Share premium		5,000
	Issue of 20,000 ordinary shares of £1 each at a premium of £0.25 per share.		
Jul. 1	6% redeemable cumulative preference shares	50,000	
	Premium on redemption of preference shares	2,500	
	Preference share redemption		52,500
	Transfer of nominal value of redeemable preference shares plus premium payable on redemption.		
	Share premium	2,500	
	Premium on redemption of preference shares		2,500
	Writing-off premium of £0.05 per share on redemption of preference shares.		
	Preference share redemption	52,500	
	Bank		52,500
	Repayment of preference shares at £1.05 per share.		
	Profit and loss	30,000	
	Capital redemption reserve		30,000
	Transfer of the nominal value of the preference shares redeemed otherwise than out of the proceeds of the new issue.		

	£	£

19X3
Sep. 30 Bonus shares   12,000
          Ordinary share capital   12,000
          Issue of one ordinary share for every ten
          shares held in accordance with Directors'
          resolution no. _____ , dated _____ .

Capital redemption reserve   12,000
          Bonus shares   12,000
          Payment of the bonus issue out of reserves.

19.4S

Barrows PLC

Journal

19X3		£	£

Jan. 31 Bank   90,000
          Application and allotment   90,000
          Amount received on application for 75,000
          ordinary shares of £1 each issued at
          £1.20 each.

Application and allotment   90,000
          Ordinary share capital   75,000
          Share premium   15,000
          Issue of 75,000 ordinary shares of £1 each
          at a premium of £0.20 per share.

Mar. 31 Redeemable share capital   100,000
Premium on redemption of share capital   10,000
          Share redemption   110,000
          Transfer of nominal value of redeemable
          shares plus premium payable on
          redemption.

Share redemption   110,000
          Bank   110,000
          Repayment of redeemable shares at
          £1.10 per share.

Profit and loss   10,000
          Premium on redemption of share
          capital   10,000
          Writing-off premium of £0.10 per share
          on redemption.

Profit and loss   25,000
          Capital redemption reserve   25,000
          Transfer of the nominal value of the shares
          redeemed otherwise than out of the
          proceeds of the new issue.

Barrows PLC

Journal

19X3		£	£
Mar. 31	Redeemable share capital	100,000	
	Premium on redemption of share capital	10,000	
	Share redemption		110,000
	Transfer of nominal value of redeemable shares plus premium payable on redemption.		
	Share redemption	110,000	
	Bank		110,000
	Repayment of redeemable shares at £1.10 per share.		
	Share premium	5,000	
	Profit and loss	5,000	
	Premium on redemption of share capital		10,000
	Writing-off premium of £0.10 per share on redemption.		

(b) The whole of the premium on redemption of share capital would be debited to the share premium account since the aggregate of the premiums received on the issue of the shares redeemed would be less than the current amount of the company's share premium account after the premium received on the issue of the new shares had been credited to that account.

The journal entry would be:

19X3		£	£
Mar. 31	Share premium	10,000	
	Premium on redemption of share capital		10,000
	Writing-off premium of £0.10 per share on redemption.		

19.6S Tutorial note

Where a company purchases its own shares out of the distributable profits, the premium payable on purchase is also paid out of the distributable profits. In the answer to part (a) therefore, the share premium account is not affected.

But where a company purchases its own shares out of the proceeds of a fresh issue of shares made for the purposes of the purchase, the premium payable on the purchase shall be paid out of the share premium account subject to the limitations given in the text – see pages 301 and 302.

(a) *Workings*

Cash		£
Balance before purchase of shares		112,000
less Cost of shares		90,000
		22,000

Capital redemption reserve		
Nominal value of shares purchased		50,000

Profit and loss account		
Balance before purchase of shares		144,000
less transfer to capital redemption reserve	50,000	
Premium on purchase	40,000	90,000
		54,000

Vincent Ganley PLC

Balance Sheet as at 31 March 19X5 (summarised)

Assets	£	£
Fixed assets		421,400
Current assets (excluding cash)	370,720	
Cash at bank	22,000	
	392,720	
less Current liabilities	260,120	132,600
		554,000
Financed by		
Share capital – issued and fully paid		
Ordinary shares		300,000
'A' ordinary shares		50,000
		350,000
Capital redemption reserve		50,000
Share premium		100,000
Profit and loss account		54,000
		554,000

(b)

Vincent Ganley PLC
Balance Sheet as at 31 March 19X5 (summarised)

Assets	£	£
Fixed assets		421,400
Current assets (excluding cash)	370,720	
Cash at bank	122,000	
	492,720	
less Current liabilities	260,120	232,600
		654,000
Financed by		
Share capital – issued and fully paid		
Ordinary shares		350,000
'A' ordinary shares		50,000
		400,000
Share premium		125,000
Profit and loss account		129,000
		654,000

The journal entries are given below:

	£	£
Bank account	100,000	
Ordinary share application account		100,000
Cash received on application for 50,000 shares of £2 each.		
Ordinary share application account	100,000	
Ordinary share capital account		50,000
Share premium account		50,000
Allotment of fresh issue of shares and transfer of premium received.		
'A' ordinary share capital account	50,000	
Premium on purchase of shares account	40,000	
'A' ordinary share purchase account		90,000
Transfer of the nominal value of the shares purchased plus premium payable.		
'A' ordinary share purchase account	90,000	
Bank account		90,000
Purchase of 50,000 'A' ordinary shares of £1 each at a premium of £0.80 per share.		
Share premium account	25,000	
Profit and loss account	15,000	
Premium on purchase of shares account		40,000
Transfer of premium on purchase of 50,000 'A' ordinary shares of £1 each. (Share premium account is debited in this case with the aggregate of the premiums received by the company on the issue of the shares redeemed because this figure is less than the current amount of the company's share premium account.)		

153

19.7S (a) Calculation of the permissible capital payment

	£
Purchase price of shares – 20,000 × £1.25	25,000
less Distributable profits	4,000
Permissible capital payment	21,000

	£
Calculation of available excess	
Nominal value of shares purchased	20,000
Permissible capital payment	21,000
Available excess	1,000

(b) Where there are no proceeds from a new issue of shares and the permissible capital payment exceeds the nominal value of the shares redeemed or purchased:

(a)   the capital redemption reserve;
(b)   the share premium account;
(c)   the company's fully paid share capital;
(d)   the amount of the company's revaluation reserve set up under paragraph 34 of Schedule 8 to the 1948 Act

may be reduced by an amount not exceeding (or by amounts not in the aggregate exceeding) the excess.

20 The issue and redemption of debentures

20.1S (a)

J. Pilling and Co. Ltd
Bank

19X2		£	
Jul. 1	9% debenture application – cash received on application	95,000	

9% debentures application

19X2		£	19X2		£
Jul. 1	9% debentures	95,000	Jul. 1	Bank – cash received on application	95,000
		95,000			95,000

9% debentures

19X2		£	19X2		£
Jul. 1	Balance c/d	100,000	Jul. 1	9% debentures application	95,000
				Discount on debentures	5,000
		100,000			100,000
			Jul. 1	Balance b/d	100,000

Discount on debentures

19X2		£	
Jul. 1	9% debentures	5,000	

(b) *Balance Sheet (extract) as at 30 June 19X3*

	£	£
Assets		
Sundry assets		X
Discount on debentures not yet written off		4,750
		X

155

		£
Financed by		
Share capital		X
Reserves		X
		—
Shareholders' funds		X
9% debentures		100,000
		—
		X
		===

20.2S (a)

Craft Ltd
Preference share redemption

19X6		£	19X6		£
May 1	Bank	132,000	May 1	7% redeemable preference shares	120,000
				Premium on redemption of preference shares	12,000
		132,000			132,000

Profit and loss

19X6		£	19X6		£
May 1	Premium on redemption of preference shares	12,000	May 1	Balance b/d	226,000
	Capital redemption reserve fund	120,000		General reserve	80,000
	Balance c/d	174,000			
		306,000			306,000
			May 1	Balance b/d	120,000

Capital redemption reserve fund

			19X6		£
			May 1	Profit and loss	174,000

Bank

19X6		£	19X6		£
May 1	Balance b/d	204,000	May 1	Preference share redemption	132,000
May 1	7½% debentures applications	147,000	May 1	Balance c/d	219,000
		351,000			351,000
May 1	Balance b/d	219,000			

7½% debentures application

19X6	£	19X6	£
May 1 7½% debentures	147,000	May 1 Bank	147,000

7½% debentures 19X0/19X2

19X6	£	19X6	£
May 1 Balance c/d	150,000	May 1 7½% debentures applications	147,000
		Discount on debentures	3,000
	150,000		150,000
		May 1 Balance b/d	150,000

Discount on debentures

19X6	£		
May 1 7½% debentures	3,000		

(b) *Balance Sheet as at 1 May 19X6*

	£	£
Assets		
Fixed assets		429,000
Current assets		
Sundry	200,000	
Bank	219,000	
	419,000	
less Current liabilities	127,000	
Net current assets		292,000
		721,000
	£	£
Financed by		
Share capital – issued and fully paid		
280,000 ordinary shares of £1 each		280,000
Reserves		
Capital redemption reserve fund	120,000	
Profit and loss account	174,000	294,000
		574,000
less Debenture discount not yet written off		3,000
Shareholders' funds		571,000
7½% debentures 19X0/19X2		150,000
		721,000

Tutorial notes
1. It has been assumed that the general reserve had been built up for the purposes of the redemption of the preference shares.
2. Note the treatment in this example of the balance on the discount on debentures account.

20.3S (a)

Switch Ltd
Journal

19X1	£	£
Bank	120,000	
Ordinary share application and allotment		120,000
Amount received on application for 200,000 ordinary shares of £0.50 each offered at £0.60 each.		
Ordinary share application and allotment	120,000	
Ordinary share capital		100,000
Share premium		20,000
Issue of 200,000 ordinary shares of £0.50 each at a premium of £0.10 per share.		
Bank	145,500	
9% Unsecured loan stock 19X5/19X4 application		145,500
Amount received on application for £150,000 9% unsecured loan stock 19X5/19X4 offered at 97.		
9% unsecured loan stock 19X5/19X4 application	145,500	
Discount on loan stock	4,500	
9% unsecured loan stock 19X5/19X4		150,000
Issue of £150,000 9% unsecured loan stock 19X5/19X4 at 97.		
6½% redeemable preference shares	175,000	
Premium on redemption of preference shares	8,750	
Preference share redemption		183,750
Transfer of nominal value of redeemable preference shares plus premium payable on redemption.		
Share premium	13,250	
Discount on loan stock		4,500
Premium on redemption of preference shares		8,750
Writing-off discount on loan stock and premium on redemption of preference shares.		
Preference share redemption	183,750	
Bank		183,750
Repayment of preference shares at £1.05 per share.		
Profit and loss	75,000	
Capital redemption reserve fund		75,000
Transfer of the nominal value of the preference shares redeemed otherwise than out of the proceeds of the new issue.		

158

(b)   *Balance Sheet as at 1 July 19X1*
                      (after completing the above entries)
	£	£
Assets		
Sundry assets		562,850
Cash at bank (Note 1)		58,500
		621,350
less Sundry creditors		19,600
Net assets		601,750
Financed by		
Share capital – issued and fully paid		
700,000 ordinary shares of £0.50 each		350,000
Reserves		
Capital redemption reserve fund	75,000	
Share premium	6,750	
Profit and loss account	20,000	101,750
Shareholders' funds		451,750
9% unsecured loan stock 19X5/19X4		150,000
		601,750

Note

1. Cash at bank

	£	£
Received from issues of:		
Ordinary shares		120,000
9% unsecured loan stock		145,500
		265,500
less Redemption of preference shares	183,750	
Overdraft brought down	23,250	207,000
		58,500

20.4S (a)   *Tapical Ltd*
                            Journal

19X7	£	£
Apr. 30 Share premium	90,000	
Profit and loss account	410,000	
Ordinary share bonus issue		500,000
Transfer of reserves for bonus issue in		
accordance with resolution no. _____,		
of the Annual General Meeting held on		
_____ 19X7.		
Ordinary share bonus issue	500,000	
Ordinary share capital		500,000
Issue of bonus shares.		

		£	£
Bank		936,000	
	Application and allotment		936,000

Amount received on application for one for four rights issue at £0.52 per share for 1.8 million shares.

		£	£
Bank		120,000	
	Application and allotment		120,000

Amount received on sale of 200,000 shares at £0.60 per share – rights issues renounced.

		£	£
Application and allotment		16,000	
	Bank		16,000

Amount of £0.08 per share on 200,000 shares paid to shareholders who renounced their rights to the rights issue.

		£	£
Application and allotment		1,040,000	
	Ordinary share capital		500,000
	Share premium		540,000

Rights issue of 2 million ordinary shares of £0.25 each at a premium of £0.27 per share.

		£	£
Issue expenses		53,000	
	Bank		53,000

Payment of underwriting and other expenses connected with the issue.

		£	£
Share premium		53,000	
	Issue expenses		53,000

Writing off issue expenses.

		£	£
Loan stock purchase		51,220	
	Bank		51,220

Payment for purchase of £60,000 loan stock.

		£	£
7½% redeemable loan stock 19X7/19X2		60,000	
Loan stock interest		1,500	
	Loan stock purchase		51,220
	Profit and loss account		10,280

Cancellation of loan stock purchased and transfer of interest on that stock to date of purchase, i.e. 4 months' interest.

160

(b) Before the one-for-four rights issue, the theoretical price of each £0.25 share was

$$\frac{\text{£4,940,000 (net assets)}}{\text{8,000,000 (shares in issue)}} = \text{£0.62 per share.}$$

After the rights issue, the theoretical price of each £0.25 share was

$$\frac{\text{£5,980,000 (net assets)}}{\text{10,000,000 (shares in issue)}} = \text{£0.60 per share.}$$

It can be seen that the theoretical price has fallen by £0.02 per share following the rights issue. The payment of £16,000 to the 0.8 million shareholders who renounced their rights is compensation for the fall in the theoretical price – (0.8m × £0.02 = £16,000).

21 Stock valuation

21.1S Smith

(a) Methods of computing the cost of stock on hand are as follows:

(i) *First in, first out (FIFO)* Under this method, stock which is received first is regarded as being issued to production, or sold, first. For valuation purposes, the stock remaining at the end of the period will be deemed to be those goods which are the last to have been purchased.

(ii) *Last in, first out (LIFO)* Under this method, stock which is received last is regarded as being issued to production, or sold, first. For valuation purposes, therefore, the stock remaining at the end of the period will be deemed to be those goods which are the first to have been purchased.

(iii) *Average cost (AVCO)* Under this method, a new average unit cost of stock is calculated whenever there is a *receipt* of goods. The latest average unit cost so calculated is used for valuation purposes at the end of the accounting period.

(b) Effect of each method on Smith's results for the six months:

	Tons	FIFO £	FIFO £	LIFO £	LIFO £	AVCO £	AVCO £
Sales	1٤ ا		4,600		4,600		4,600
Cost of sales:							
Purchases	140	5,600		5,600		5,600	
less Closing stock	40	1,715	3,885	1,560	4,040	1,600	4,000
	100						
Gross profit			715		560		600

Comments

In times of rising prices, stock valued by the FIFO method will give both a higher closing stock valuation and a higher profit than stock valued by the LIFO method. Both methods have disadvantages: under FIFO sales are matched with purchases valued at out of date prices whilst under LIFO that part of the stock below which the level

162

never falls could be valued at the prices which applied when the business commenced.

The AVCO method has the advantage of smoothing out fluctuations in the purchase price of goods and will usually result in a profit somewhere between the FIFO and LIFO figures.

Perhaps the most important point to make, however, is that whatever method of stock valuation is adopted, that method should be applied consistently.

Workings

1. Purchases

	Tons	Price per ton £	Value £
1 July	20	38	760
5 August	30	40	1,200
12 September	25	35	875
20 October	40	42	1,680
11 November	15	43	645
10 December	10	44	440
	140		5,600

2. Closing stock valuation

   (i) FIFO

	£
10 tons at £44	440
15 tons at £43	645
15 tons at £42	630
40 tons	1,715

   (ii) LIFO

	£
20 tons at £38	760
20 tons at £40	800
40 tons	1,560

   (iii) AVCO

$$\frac{\text{Total cost}}{\text{Total units}} = \frac{£5,600}{140 \text{ tons}} = £40 \text{ per ton}$$

Stock = 40 tons at £40 per ton = £1,600

21.2S (a) Valuation of closing stock

Transaction				Stock remaining					
				Valued at LIFO			Valued at FIFO		
		Units	Unit price £	Units	Unit price	£	Units	Unit price	£
Jan.	Bought	30	5	30	5	150	30	5	150
	Sold	20		10	5	50	10	5	50
Feb.	Sold	5		5	5	25	5	5	25
Apr.	Bought	40	6	40	6	240	40	6	240
				5	5	25			
	Sold	25		15	6	90	20	6	120
May	Bought	25	6.5	25	6.5	162.5	25	6.5	162.5
				5	5	25			
	Sold	30		10	6	60	15	6.5	97.5
Jun.	Bought	20	7	20	7	140	20	7	140
				5	5	25			
	Sold	20		10	6	60	15	7	105
Closing stock						85			105

Gross profit

	LIFO basis		FIFO basis	
	£	£	£	£
Sales		811.00		811.00
Cost of sales				
Purchases	692.50		692.50	
less Closing stock	85.00	607.50	105.00	587.50
Gross profit		203.50		223.50

(b) Balance Sheets as at 30 June 19X5

	LIFO basis £	FIFO basis £
Assets		
Stock at cost	85.00	105.00
Cash	618.50	618.50
	703.50	723.50
Financed by		
Capital account		
Amount introduced	500.00	500.00
Profit for period	203.50	223.50
	703.50	723.50

Comments

In times of rising prices, which obtained during the six month period covered by the question, the FIFO valuation can be seen to give a higher closing stock valuation and a higher profit. The disadvantage of using the FIFO basis, that sales are matched with purchases valued at out of date prices, must be stressed as indeed must the disadvantage of an outdated stock valuation using the LIFO basis.

21.3S (a)

Weighted average method (AVCO)

Date	Purchases			Issues			Balance		
	Quantity	Price £	Value £	Quantity	Price £	Value £	Quantity	Price £	Value £
b/f							100	39	3,900
May	100	41	4,100				200	40	8,000
Jun.	200	50	10,000				400	45	18,000
Jul.				250	45	11,250	150	45	6,750
Aug.	400	51.875	20,750				550	50	27,500
Sep.				350	50	17,500	200	50	10,000
Oct.				100	50	5,000	100	50	5,000

FIFO method

Date	Purchases			Issues			Balance		
	Quantity	Price £	Value £	Quantity	Price £	Value £	Quantity	Price £	Value £
b/f							100	39	3,900
May	100	41	4,100				100	41	4,100
Jun.	200	50	10,000				200	50	10,000
Jul.				100	39	3,900			
				100	41	4,100			
				50	50	2,500	150	50	7,500
Aug.	400	51.875	20,750				400	51.875	20,750
Sep.				150	50	7,500			
				200	51.875	10,375	200	51.875	10,375
Oct.				100	51.875	5,187.5	100	51.875	5,187.5

LIFO method

Date	Purchases			Issues			Balance		
	Quantity	Price £	Value £	Quantity	Price £	Value £	Quantity	Price £	Value £
b/f							100	39	3,900
May	100	41	4,100				100	41	4,100
Jun.	200	50	10,000				200	50	10,000
Jul.				200	50	10,000	100	39	3,900
				50	41	2,050	50	41	2,050
Aug.	400	51.875	20,750				100	39	3,900
							50	41	2,050
							400	51.875	20,750
Sep.				350	51.875	18,156.25	100	39	3,900
							50	41	2,050
							50	51.875	2593.75
Oct.				50	51.875	2593.75			
				50	41	2,050	100	39	3,900

(b) *Trading Accounts for the 6 months to 31 October 19XX*

	Weighted average method		FIFO method		LIFO method	
	£	£	£	£	£	£
Sales		47,900		47,900		47,900
Cost of sales:						
Opening stock	3,900		3,900		3,900	
Purchases	34,850		34,850		34,850	
	38,750		38,750		38,750	
less Closing stock	5,000	33,750	5,187.5	33,562.5	3,900	34,850
Gross profit		14,150		14,337.5		13,050

(c) The method, in the situation depicted, which is regarded as giving the best method of profit, is the LIFO method. When prices are rising the LIFO method matches the sales receipts with up to date costs of the goods sold.

Working
Sales

		£
Jul.	250 units at £64	16,000
Sep.	350 units at £70	24,500
Oct.	100 units at £74	7,400
		47,900

	Product A £	B £	C £
Sales – actual prices	172,500	159,400	74,600
add Discounts	2,500	600	400
	175,000	160,000	75,000
less Gross profit on normal selling prices	35,000	40,000	25,000
Cost of sales	140,000	120,000	50,000

(a) Values of stock at 31 December 19X7

	A £	B £	C £
Stock at 1 January 19X7	24,000	36,000	12,000
Purchases	146,000	124,000	48,000
	170,000	160,000	60,000
less Cost of sales	140,000	120,000	50,000
Stock at 31 December 19X7	30,000	40,000	10,000

(b) Gross profit by product

	A £	B £	C £
Sales – actual prices	172,500	159,400	74,600
less Cost of sales	140,000	120,000	50,000
Actual gross profit	32,500	39,400	24,600

22 Funds flow statements; cash budgeting

J. Cook

*Statement of Source and Application of Funds
for the year ended 31 December 19X2*

	£	£
Source of funds		
Profits for year		9,200
add Depreciation		1,150
Total from operations		10,350
Application of funds		
Drawings	8,890	
Purchase of fixed assets	1,500	10,390
		(40)
Increase/decrease in working capital		
Increase in stocks	100	
Increase in debtors	30	
(Increase) in creditors	(60)	
(Decrease) in bank	(100)	
(Decrease) in cash	(10)	(40)

Workings

Calculation of working capital

	£ 19X1	£ 19X2	£ Increase (+) or decrease (−) in working capital
Current assets			
Stock	2,100	2,200	+ 100
Debtors	370	400	+ 30
Bank	1,200	1,100	− 100
Cash	140	130	− 10
	3,810	3,830	+ 20
Current liabilities			
Creditors	430	490	− 60
	3,380	3,340	− 40

D. Riggs
Funds Flow Statement
for the year ended 31 December 19X3

	£	£
Source of funds		
Profits for year		16,225
Depreciation		6,200
Total from operations		22,425
Application of funds		
Drawings	11,795	
Purchase of fixed assets	14,400	26,195
		(3,770)
Increase/decrease in working capital		
Increase in stocks	850	
Increase in debtors	1,020	
Increase in cash	60	
(Increase) in creditors	(58)	1,872
Decrease in bank balances		5,642

Workings
Calculations of working capital

	£ 19X1	£ 19X2	£ Increase/ decrease
Current assets			
Stock	1,100	1,950	+ 850
Debtors	270	1,290	+ 1,020
Bank	1,320		− 1,320
Cash	370	430	+ 60
	3,060	3,670	+ 610
Current liabilities			
Creditors	793	851	− 58
Bank		4,322	− 4,322
	793	5,173	− 4,380
	2,267	−1,503	− 3,770

MacDonalds Ltd
Flow of Funds Statement for 19X4

	£000	£000
Source of funds		
Profit before tax and *before depreciation*		643
		——
Total from operations		643
Funds from other sources		
Sale of 10% debentures	150	
Sale of plant and machinery	17	167
		——
		810
Application of funds		
Dividends paid	40	
Tax paid	150	
Purchase of plant and machinery	1,150	1,340
		——
		(530)
Increase/decrease in working capital		
Increase in stock	75	
Increase in debtors	180	
(Increase) in creditors	(120)	
(Decrease) in bank	(665)	(530)
		——

(b) A funds flow statement identifies the movement in assets, liabilities and capital which have taken place during a particular year and the resultant effect on net liquid funds. This information is not readily discernible from a profit and loss account and/or balance sheet.

Workings
1. Calculation of working capital

	£ 19X3	£ 19X4	£ Increase/ decrease
Current assets			
Stock	510	585	+ 75
Debtors	900	1,080	+ 180
Bank	690	25	− 665
	——	——	——
	2,100	1,690	− 410
	——	——	
Current liabilities			
Creditors	360	480	− 120
	——	——	——
	1,740	1,210	− 530
	══	══	══

2. Profit before tax 19X4

	£
Trading profit	970
less Expenses	327
	643

3. Fixed assets (plant, etc.)

	Cost	
	£	£
Balance 19X4		1,735
Deduct 19X3	655	
less Sales	70	585
Purchases 19X4		1,150

22.4S This question only requests sources of finance, but it is suggested that a source and application of funds statement would provide a more satisfactory solution together with the note.

GLS Limited
Source and Application of Funds Statement
for the year ended 31 August 19X8

	£000	£000
Source of funds		
Profit before tax		100
add Depreciation		71
Total from operations		171
Funds from other sources		
Sale of investments	80	
Sale of fixed assets	200	
Issue of preference shares	50	
Issue of ordinary shares (including premium)	100	
Issue of debentures	100	
Loan from ICFC	50	
Government grant	20	600
		771
Application of funds		
Tax paid	60	
Purchase of plant and equipment	900	
Purchase of leasehold land and buildings	50	1,010
		(239)
Increase/decrease in working capital		
(Decrease) in stock	(100)	
(Increase) in creditors	(35)	
(Decrease) in bank	(104)	(239)

The question requires 'sources of finance' only. If SSAP 10 were to be adhered to, only the section headed 'Source of funds' would be necessary to comply with the question. However, the decrease in working capital could be regarded as a source of finance. A full source and application of funds statement is therefore provided.

Workings

1. Working capital

	£000 19X7	£000 19X8	£000 Increase/ decrease
Current assets			
Stocks and work in progress	300	200	− 100
Debtors	100	100	
Bank	10	(94)	− 104
	410	206	− 204
Current liabilities			
Creditors (including acceptance credits)	40	75	− 35
	370	131	− 239

2. Profits before tax

	£
Increase in retained profits	40
Taxation	60
	100

Note: This must assume no dividends have been paid

3. Depreciation

	£
Increase in depreciation on leases	1
on plant, etc.	70
	71

4. Issue of ordinary shares

	£	£
Balance 19X8		320
less Balance 19X7	200	
add Bonus (1 for 5)	40	240
		80
add Premium of 25%		20
Issue for cash		100

22.9S   *Cash budget for period January to June 19X2*

	Jan. £	Feb. £	Mar. £	Apr. £	May £	Jun. £
Receipts						
Cash sales	30,000	28,000	24,000	32,000	29,000	36,000
Credit sales[1]	62,000	68,000	78,000	64,000	84,000	74,000
	92,000	96,000	102,000	96,000	113,000	110,000
Payments						
Purchases	26,000	25,000	30,000	30,000	25,000	25,000
Expenses	15,000	12,000	18,000	20,000	18,000	20,000
Wages	40,000	40,000	40,000	40,000	40,000	40,000
Rates				15,000		
Interest						10,000
Dividend						30,000
	81,000	77,000	88,000	105,000	83,000	125,000
Cash increase/ (decrease) during month	11,000	19,000	14,000	(9,000)	30,000	(15,000)
Cash brought forward	6,000					
Closing cash	17,000	36,000	50,000	41,000	71,000	56,000

Note
1. Credit sales

80% previous	48,000	56,000	64,000	48,000	72,000	56,000
20% penult.	14,000	12,000	14,000	16,000	12,000	18,000
	62,000	68,000	78,000	64,000	84,000	74,000

Cash budget for period January to April

	Jan. £	Feb. £	Mar. £	Apr. £
Receipts				
Sales (Note 1)	62,000	49,500	46,000	62,000
Payments				
Purchases	50,000	78,000	84,000	84,000
Wages	5,000	5,200	5,200	5,000
Expenses	4,000	8,000	6,000	6,000
	59,000	91,200	95,200	95,000
Cash increase/(decrease) during month	3,000	(41,700)	(49,200)	(33,000)
Cash brought forward	9,000			
Closing cash-in-hand/ (overdrawn)	12,000	(29,700)	(78,900)	(111,900)

Note

1. Sales

½ previous	30,500	19,000	27,000	35,000
½ penult.	31,500	30,500	19,000	27,000
	62,000	49,500	46,000	62,000

Cash receipts in May should amount to £75,000 (½ of March plus ½ of April sales). Cash payments will be for April purchases and expenses, i.e. £65,000 plus May wages. From the information provided for previous months it appears that May wages will be approximately £5,000. The cash position in May should therefore improve by about £5,000.

An alternative way of dealing with this part of the question would be to extend the cash budget to include May. A footnote would then be required to explain any assumed figures, and to draw conclusions from the tabulation.

(a)   *Schubert Ltd*

Cash budget for period April to June 19X5

	Apr. £	May £	Jun. £
Receipts			
Credit sales	1,500	1,800	2,000
Cash sales	500	600	800
	2,000	2,400	2,800
Payments			
Trade creditors	4,000	2,300	2,700
Wages	300	300	300
Administration	150	150	150
Rent	360		
Dividend			1,500
Equipment	1,600		
	6,410	2,750	4,650
Cash brought forward	3,500	(910)	(1,260)
Cash increase/(decrease) during month	(4,410)	(350)	(1,850)
Closing cash/(overdrawn)	(910)	(1,260)	(3,110)

(b)   *Schubert Ltd*

Projected Trading and Profit and Loss Account for period April to June 19X5

	£	£
Sales		
Cash	1,900	
Credit	6,300	8,200
Cost of sales		
Opening stock	2,000	
Purchases	7,600	
	9,600	
less Closing stock (Note 1)	3,450	6,150
Gross profit (Note 1)		2,050
less Expenses		
Wages	900	
Administration	450	
Rent	90	
Depreciation	75	1,515
		535

175

Notes
1. Gross profit = 25% of Sales (£8,200) = £2,050.
   Cost of Sales = Sales (£8,200) less gross profit (£2,050)
                    = £6,150.
   Closing stock = Cost of sales (£6,150) deducted from total of
              Opening stock (£2,000) and Purchases (£7,600) = £3,450.
2. There is a loss on the sale of the replaced equipment amounting to
   £100. This loss could be charged to this period, but would
   more likely be charged against the full year.

(c) At the commencement of the period, cash in hand amounted to
£3,500, whereas at the end cash will be overdrawn £3,110, a reduction in cash of £6,610.
The reasons for the difference between budgeted profitability and
budgeted liquidity are probably best explained by a flow statement:

Statement	£	£
Source of funds (i.e. cash)		
Profits		535
Depreciation		75
Total generated from operations		610
Application of funds (i.e. cash)		
Dividends paid	1,500	
Purchase of equipment	1,600	3,100
Increase/(decrease) in working capital		(2,490)
Increase in stocks	1,450	
Increase in debtors (Note 1)	1,000	
Increase in prepayment (Note 3)	270	
Decrease in creditors (Note 2)	1,400	4,120
Increase/(decrease) in cash		(6,610)

In simple terms, it would appear that profits should produce a cash
increase of £535, plus depreciation of £75 (depreciation is a non-cash
expense), i.e. £610. However, cash has been paid out on dividends
(£1,500) and equipment (£1,600). Stocks have also been increased,
so decreasing cash, as have debtors and prepayments. Creditors have
been reduced, again decreasing cash.

Notes
1. Debtors have increased from £1,500 to £2,500.
2. Creditors have decreased from £4,000 to £2,600.
3. The prepayment is for rent paid nine months in advance.

23 Interpretation of accounts – an introduction

23.1S   *R. J. Smith*

(a) 'Gross profit ratio' means the ratio of gross profit to net sales. It shows the percentage mark-up on selling price.

(b) (i) $\dfrac{5,250}{21,000} \times 100 = 25\%$

(ii) $\dfrac{2,412}{21,000} \times 100 = 11.5\%$

(iii) $\dfrac{420}{21,000} \times 100 = 2\%$

(iv) £18,000, i.e. opening stock plus purchases

(v) £15,750, i.e. opening stock plus purchases less closing stock

(c)   *Budgeted Trading and Profit and Loss Account*
              for the year to 31 March 19X6

		£	£
	Sales		23,100
	less Cost of sales		17,325
(i)	Gross profit		5,775
	less Rent and rates	800	
	Light and heat	192	
	Wages	936	
	Part-time salesman's commission	462	
	Delivery expenses	230	
	Depreciation of fittings	120	
	Office and sundry expenses	390	3,130
(ii)	Net profit		2,645

23.2S (a)

S. Ltd and T. Ltd

		S. Ltd	T. Ltd
(i)	Net profit as a percentage of net assets	$\frac{8,000}{100,000} \times 100 = 8\%$	$\frac{6,000}{50,000} \times 100 = 12\%$
(ii)	Net profit as a percentage of sales	$\frac{8,000}{160,000} \times 100 = 5\%$	$\frac{6,000}{120,000} \times 100 = 5\%$
(iii)	Gross profit as a percentage of sales	$\frac{64,000}{160,000} \times 100 = 40\%$	$\frac{45,000}{120,000} \times 100 = 37.5\%$
(iv)	Current assets to current liabilities	$90,000 : 30,000 = 3 : 1$	$60,000 : 30,000 = 2 : 1$
(v)	Debtors and cash to current liabilities	$33,000 : 30,000 = 1.1 : 1$	$30,000 : 30,000 = 1 : 1$
(vi)	Cost of sales to average stock held	$96,000 : 48,000 = 2 : 1$	$75,000 : 25,000 = 3 : 1$

In item (vi) above, average stock is taken as (Opening stock + Closing stock) ÷ 2.

(b) S. Ltd obtains a higher gross profit percentage than T. Ltd, but since the net profit percentage of both companies is the same the overhead expenses of T. Ltd must be lower than those of S. Ltd by a compensating amount.

The return on capital employed by T. Ltd is half as much again higher than that of S. Ltd. The reason for this better performance is shown in the other ratios:

  (i) The stock of T. Ltd is turned over three times a year compared to S. Ltd's twice.

 (ii) T. Ltd's cover of current liabilities by current assets of 2 : 1 is adequate.

(iii) S. Ltd has more investment in stocks than necessary: the money so tied up could be more profitably invested. Both companies' 'acid test' ratio is satisfactory.

23.3S

Report to the directors of Unigear Ltd

February 19X3

Gentlemen,

We submit our report on the results for the year ended 31 December 19X2, and a comparison with those of the previous year.

1. *Summary of results* A brief summary of the results of the two years shows the following:

	19X2		19X1	
	%	£	%	£
Sales	100	1,000,000	100	1,500,000
Cost of sales	65	650,000	60	900,000

	%	19X2 £	%	19X1 £
Gross profit	35	350,000	40	600,000
Overhead expenses	34.3	343,098	26.3	394,704
Net profit before tax	0.7	6,902	13.7	205,296
Corporation tax	0.3	3,000	3.8	57,500
Net profit after tax	0.4	3,902	9.9	147,796

The reduction in overhead expenses is accounted for, viz.

	19X2 £	19X1 £	Net £
Decreases:			
Directors' remuneration	24,650	67,740	43,090
Wages and salaries	187,724	233,719	45,995
Repairs and renewals	750	2,600	1,850
	213,124	304,059	90,935
Increases:			
Rent and rates	12,106	10,450	1,656
Light and heat	4,942	3,608	1,334
Advertising	42,605	40,216	2,389
Bad debts	12,943	4,224	8,719
Bank interest and commission	46,420	22,328	24,092
Other expenses	10,958	9,819	1,139
	129,974	90,645	39,329
Net decrease			51,606

2. *Observations on the results*

(a) *Trading account*   Sales have fallen from £1.5m to £1m – a reduction of one-third. The probable reason for this reduction is the nature of the trade in which your company is engaged.

Gross profit percentage has fallen from 40% to 35%. This reduction may be attributable to the following reasons:

(i) Deliberate reductions in selling prices in order to stimulate sales

(ii) A change in the goods sold – more sales of those goods with lower mark-ups

(iii) Losses from pilferage of stock and/or cash

(iv) Significant mark down of stock at 31 December 19X2 resulting in a higher cost of sales figure for that year.

The rate of stock turnover has decreased. Assuming that the average stock reflects the general stock levels during the year and that the sales accrue evenly over the year, the decrease can be shown as follows:

179

	19X2	19X1
Average of opening and closing stocks	£355,000	£275,000
Cost of goods sold	£650,000	£900,000
Number of times stock turned over	1.8 times	3.3 times
Number of months sales in stock, at cost	6.6 months	3.6 months

It is obvious that stock levels have increased substantially during the current year. Holding stocks is an expense which should be reduced as soon as possible by reviewing the company's stock lines if necessary. In view of the nature of the business, it must be ensured that the stock at 31 December 19X2 is valued at the lower of cost or net realisable value for each line held.

(b) *Profit and loss account*   The decrease in directors' remuneration and wages and salaries obviously reflect the lower levels of business.

The increase in bad debts would suggest that the credit control procedures need reviewing as a matter of urgency.

Bank interest and commission has increased by a substantial amount and part of this must be due to the high cost of maintaining stock levels referred to earlier and part to capital expenditure (see below).

3. *Corporation tax*   The adjusted corporation tax charge for 19X1 represents 28% of the net profit. Obviously, considerable capital expenditure relief was available to reduce the rate below the normal corporation tax rate. The cost of these new assets must have been financed by bank borrowing since no loan or hire purchase interest payable is shown in the accounts. In view of this, it is surprising to see a reduction in the depreciation charge for the current year. Perhaps this figure will need to be adjusted.

4. *Dividends*   No dividend is proposed for the current year.

We shall be pleased to discuss the contents of our report with you in detail.

Yours faithfully,

23.4S (a)

The Alpha Co. Ltd
Appropriation Account
for the year ended 31 December 19X5

	£	£	£
Net profit for the year			72,000
Unappropriated profit brought forward			73,000
			145,000

	£	£	£
Appropriation of profit:			
Transfer to general reserve		25,000	
Dividends:			
Paid – Interim preference – 4%	10,000		
Interim ordinary – 5%	5,000	15,000	
Proposed – Final preference – 4%	10,000		
Final ordinary – 5%	5,000	15,000	
Goodwill written off		20,000	
			75,000
Unappropriated profit carried forward			70,000

Balance Sheet as at 31 December 19X5

Assets

	Cost or valuation* £	Depreciation £	Net £
Fixed assets			
Land and buildings	270,000*	–	270,000
Fittings	175,000	75,000	100,000
Motor vehicles	397,000	187,000	210,000
	842,000	262,000	580,000
Goodwill not yet written off			40,000
Current assets			
Stock		148,000	
Debtors (Note)		83,000	
Short term investments			
(market value £43,000)		39,000	
		270,000	
less Current liabilities			
Creditors	48,000		
Bank overdraft	27,000		
Proposed dividends	15,000	90,000	
Net current assets			180,000
			800,000

Financed by	Authorised	Issued and fully paid
Share capital		
8% £1 redeemable preference shares	250,000	250,000
£1 ordinary shares	200,000	100,000
	450,000	350,000

	£	£
Reserves		
Capital redemption reserve	150,000	
Revaluation reserve	50,000	
Share premium	20,000	
General reserve	80,000	
Profit and loss account	70,000	370,000
Shareholders' funds		720,000
Loan capital		
10% debentures		80,000
		800,000

Note
Debtors

	£
Trade debtors and prepayments	85,400
less Provision for doubtful debts	2,400
	83,000

(b) (1) The balance of the share capital can be issued by the company at any time it wishes to raise additional finance.

(2) Return on net capital employed is given by

Net profit for the year + Debenture interest ÷ Net capital employed = £72,000 + £8,000 ÷ £800,000 = 10%.

This ratio measures the overall effectiveness of the company's operations.

(3) The company's working capital (or net current assets) is £180,000. The importance of working capital is that it shows whether a company is able to meet its debts as and when they fall due.

(4) In the case of Alpha Co. Ltd, the goodwill would have arisen on the purchase of another business where the purchase price exceeded the net assets acquired.

(5) Assuming the company had the cash, the maximum amount which could be distributed by way of dividend is given as follows:

	£
Profit and loss account balance	145,000
General reserve	55,000
	200,000
less Preference dividends	20,000
	180,000

182

The other reserves are non-distributable.
(6) The market value of the shares reflects the future expectations of the business whilst the book value is based on the historic cost of the assets.
(7) The share premium account has arisen because at some time the Alpha Co. Ltd issued shares at a price above their par value.

24 Value added tax (VAT)

24.1S

J. Madden Ltd
Sales day book

Folio 5/1

Date 19X6		Folio	Total £	Sales £	VAT £
May	6 H. Smith Ltd	DS3	115	100	15
	9 R. Scruton & Co.	DS1	184	160	24
	13 R. Hollis & Co.	DH1	138	120	18
	16 E. Aldcroft Ltd	DA1	230	200	30
	20 M. Daniels & Co.	DD1	92	80	12
	23 E. Seddon & Co.	DS2	161	140	21
	27 H. Smith Ltd	DS3	207	180	27
			1,127	980	147
				NS1	CV1

Ledger

E. Aldcroft Ltd Folio DA1

19X6		Folio	£	
May 16	Sales day book	5/1	230	

M. Daniels & Co. Folio DD1

19X6		Folio	£	
May 20	Sales day book	5/1	92	

R. Hollis & Co. Folio DH1

19X6		Folio	£	
May 13	Sales day book	5/1	138	

184

R. Scruton & Co.   Folio DS1

19X6		Folio	£	
May 9	Sales day book	5/1	184	

E. Seddon & Co.   Folio DS2

19X6		Folio	£	
May 23	Sales day book	5/1	161	

H. Smith Ltd   Folio DS3

19X6		Folio	£	19X6		Folio	£
May 6	Sales day book	5/1	115	May 31	Balance c/d		322
May 27	Sales day book	5/1	207				
			322				322
Jun. 1	Balance b/d		232				

Sales   Folio NS1

				19X6		Folio	£
				May 31	Sales day book	5/1	980

Value added tax   Folio CV1

				19X6		Folio	£
				May 31	Sales day book	5/1	147

185

24.2S

Stanley Jones
Bank account

Date	£		Date		Cheque no.	Total including VAT	Shop fittings	Purchases	Motor vehicle	Cash	Light and heat	VAT
						£	£	£	£	£	£	£
19X1			19X1									
Jul. 1 Balance b/d	25,012		Jul. 1	Shop fittings		2,300	2,000					300
3 Cash	920			Purchases		9,200		8,000				1,200
10 Cash	1,035			Ford Escort UDB 95R		1,150			1,150			
17 Cash	1,127		3	Petty cash		600				600		
24 Cash	1,058		12	Norweb		240					240	
31 Cash	966		26	British Gas		115					115	
						13,605	2,000	8,000	1,150	600	355	1,500
			31	Balance c/d		16,513	NS2	NP1	NM2	¢	NL1	CV1
	30,118					30,118						
Aug. 1 Balance b/d	16,513											

Petty cash book

Debit side

Date		Total including VAT	Sales	VAT	Bank
		£	£	£	£
19X1					
Jul. 1	Takings	920	800	120	
3	Bank	600			600
8	Takings	1,035	900	135	
15	Takings	1,127	980	147	
22	Takings	1,058	920	138	
29	Takings	966	840	126	
31	Takings	92	80	12	
		5,798	4,520	678	600
			NS1	CV1	¢
		5,798			
Aug. 1	Balance b/d	97			

Credit side

Date		Total including VAT	Bank	Motor car expenses	Wages	VAT
		£	£	£	£	£
19X1						
Jul. 3	Bank	920	920			
7	Motor car expenses	23		20		3
7	Wages	120			120	
10	Bank	1,035	1,035			
14	Motor car expenses	46		40		6
14	Wages	120			120	
17	Bank	1,127	1,127			
21	Motor car expenses	23		20		3
21	Wages	120			120	
24	Bank	1,058	1,058			
28	Motor car expenses	23		20		3
28	Wages	120			120	
31	Bank	966	966			
		5,701	5,106	100	480	15
			¢	NM1	NW1	CV1
31	Balance c/d	97				
		5,798				

Light and heat — Folio NL1

19X1			£	
Jul. 31	Bank	B1	355	

Motor car expenses — Folio NM1

19X1			£	
Jul. 31	Petty cash book	CB1	100	

Motor vehicle — Folio NM2

19X1			£	
Jul. 31	Bank	B1	1,150	

Purchases — Folio NP1

19X1			£	
Jul. 31	Bank	B1	8,000	

Sales — Folio NS1

			19X1			£
			Jul. 31	Petty cash book	CB1	4,520

Shop fittings — Folio NS2

19X1			£	
Jul. 31	Bank	B1	2,000	

Wages — Folio NW1

19X1			£	
Jul. 31	Petty cash book	CB1	480	

Value added tax — Folio CV1

19X1			£	19X1			£
Jul. 31	Bank	B1	1,500	Jul. 31	Petty cash book	CB1	678
31	Petty cash book	CB1	15	31	Balance c/d		837
			1,515				1,515
Aug. 1	Balance b/d		837				

25 Suspense accounts and the correction of errors

25.1S (a)

Suspense account

Error no.		£	Error no.		£
	Trial balance	218	(i)	Bank	35
(iv)	Discounts received	426	(iii)	M. Smith	94
	Balance – unexplained		(iv)	Discounts allowed	396
	difference c/d	188	(v)	Bank	111
			(vii)	Carriage outwards	196
		832			832
				Balance b/d	188

Error (ii) will not affect the trial balance since no entries have been made in the books for the goods taken by the owner of the business.

Error (vi) will not affect the trial balance since the error is merely a switch between two debit balances.

All the above errors should be corrected by means of journal entries.

(b) The balance of a trial balance is only a check on the arithmetical accuracy of the postings to the ledger accounts and is not evidence of the absence of error. Certain types of error will not affect the trial balance, viz.

1. Errors of omission – where the transaction is completely omitted from the ledger
2. Errors of commission – where both the debit and the credit are posted but to the wrong account
3. Errors of principle – where revenue expenditure is classified as capital expenditure or vice versa
4. Compensating errors.

(a)
                              Misbal Co.
                              Journal

		£	£
1.	Suspense account	100	
	Purchase ledger control account		100
	Invoice from J. Smith omitted from control account.		
2.	Debtors control account	240	
	Sales		240
	Undercast of sales day book.		
3.	Discount allowed account	489	
	Suspense account		489
	Discount allowed not posted to nominal account.		
4.	Purchases	2,410	
	Purchase ledger control account		2,410
	Invoice from Why Ltd received late.		
5.	Sales	192	
	Sales ledger control account		192
	Cheque from J. Jones treated as sale.		
6.	Sales	250	
	Disposal of motor van account		250
	Trade in allowance wrongly treated.		

Tutorial note
It has been assumed that the difference in the trial balance figures
has been posted to a suspense account.

(b)   *Profit Adjustment Statement*

		Increase £	Decrease £
2.	Sales day book undercast	240	
3.	Discount allowed not posted		489
4.	Purchase invoice from Why Ltd		2,410
5.	Sales incorrectly credited		192
6.	Sales incorrectly credited		250
		240	3,341
			240
	Net decrease in profit		3,101

Note
Item 1 will not affect the profit.

(c)   *Trial Balance Adjustment Statement*

		Increase debit or decrease credit £	Increase credit or decrease debit £
1.	Invoice omitted from purchase ledger control account		100
3.	Discount allowed not posted	489	

	£	£
	489	100
	100	
Net difference to trial balance	389	

Tutorial note
The other items will not affect the trial balance.

25.3S (a)

ABC Limited
Journal

		£	£
(a)	Profit and loss account	350	
	Sales ledger control account		350
	Correction of rent payment debited to sales ledger control account in error.		
(f)	Profit and loss account	1,000	
	Purchases ledger control account		1,000
	Correction of cash purchase debited to purchase ledger control account.		
(i)	Difference on balances suspense account	1,900	
	Bank account		1,900
	Correction of overcast of bank debit column in March 19X0		

(b)

Corrected List of Balances at 30 April 19X0

	Note	£	£
Fixed assets: at cost	1	68,640	
provision for depreciation			31,000
Ordinary share capital			35,000
Retained earnings	2		9,930
Stock in trade, at cost		14,000	
Sales ledger control account	3	9,810	
Purchases ledger control account	4		6,240
Balance at bank	5		9,980
Difference on balance suspense	6		300
		92,450	92,450

Notes
1. Fixed assets: at cost

	£
Per list of balances	60,000
Fixtures and fittings purchased (j)	8,640
	68,640

2. Retained earnings

	£	£
Per list of balances		12,000
add Cash sales (g)		2,450
		14,450

	£	£
less Rent (a)	350	
Discounts allowed (c)	500	
Purchases (e)	300	
Purchase ledger control (f)	1,000	
Bank charges (h)	910	
Stationery (k)	1,460	4,520
		9,930

3. Sales ledger control account

	£	£
Per list of balances		9,600
add Refund to L. Green (d)		2,620
		12,220
less Rent (a)	350	
B. Bell (b)	1,560	
Discounts allowed (c)	500	2,410
		9,810

4. Purchase ledger control account

	£
Per list of balances	6,500
add Correction of purchase day book (e)	300
Payment to K. Bloom (f)	1,000
	7,800
less B. Bell (b)	1,560
	6,240

5. Bank

	£	£	
Per list of balances		1,640	in hand
add Cash sales (g)		2,450	
		4,090	
less Refund to L. Green (d)	2,620		
Bank charges (h)	910		
Overcast of debit column (i)	1,900		
Fixtures and fittings (j)	8,640	14,070	
		9,980	overdrawn

6. Difference on balance suspense account

	£	
Per list of balances	740	credit
add Stationery not posted (k)	1,460	
	2,220	
less Bank cost (i)	1,900	
	300	credit

Note

The trial balance in this question implies that the sales ledger control account and the purchases ledger control account have been regarded as an integral part of the double entry system.

(c) The reasons for preparing bank reconciliation statements are as follows:

- (i) To check that all items shown on the bank statement have been recorded in the cash book.
- (ii) To identify unpresented cheques.
- (iii) To verify the balance shown in the cash book.

25.4S (a)

Perrod and Company
Debtors control account

	£		£
Balance per schedule	1,891	Bad debts	68
Cheque returned	110	Discount allowed – M. Smith	43
Sales omitted – A. Jones	97	Balance c/d	1,987
	2,098		2,098
Balance b/d	1,987		

Creditors control account

	£		£
Invoice overstated	9	Balance per schedule	2,130
Balance c/d	2,121		
	2,130		2,130
		Balance b/d	2,121

(b) *Journal*

		£	£
(iii)	Office equipment	240	
	Purchases		240
	Invoice wrongly analysed.		
(iv)	Drawings	320	
	Wages		320
	Drawings of owner included in wages.		
(v)	Capital account	40	
	Provision for depreciation of office equipment		40
	Depreciation charge for 19X7 calculated at 10% on cost instead of 12½% on cost.		
(vi)	Drawings	45	
	Stationery		45
	Personal notepaper included in stationery.		

		£	£
(vii)	Returns inwards	90	
	Returns outwards		90
	Goods returned to a creditor posted to wrong returns account.		

(c)   *Balance Sheet as at 31 December 19X8*

Assets

	Cost	Depre-ciation	Net
	£	£	£
Fixed assets			
Premises	7,000	–	7,000
Office equipment (Note 1)	1,840	750	1,090
	8,840	750	8,090
Current assets			
Stock		1,400	
Debtors		1,987	
Cash in hand		56	
		3,443	
less Current liabilities			
Creditors	2,121		
Bank overdraft	980	3,101	
Net current assets			342
			8,432
Financed by			
Capital account			
Balance at 1 January 19X8 (Note 2)			8,400
add Profit for the year (Note 3)			2,332
			10,732
less Drawings (Note 4)			2,300
			8,432

Notes

1. Office equipment – cost

	£
Per schedule	1,600
From purchases	240
	1,840

2. Capital – balance brought forward

	£
Per schedule	8,440
less Depreciation for 19X7	40
	8,400

3. Profit for the year

	£	£	£
Sales			14,003
less Returns inwards (£310 + £90)			400
			13,603
Cost of sales			
Stock at 1 January 19X8		1,200	
Purchases (£9,480 − £240)	9,240		
less Returns outwards	90	9,150	
		10,350	
less Stock at 31 December 19X8		1,400	8,950
Gross profit			4,653
Discount received			121
			4,774
Wages (£1,540 − £320)		1,220	
Commission		160	
Heating and lighting		375	
Postage and stationery (£224 − £45)		179	
Discount allowed		210	
Bad debts		68	
Depreciation on office equipment		230	2,442
			2,332

4. Drawings

	£
Per schedule	1,935
From wages	320
From stationery	45
	2,300

26 Bills of exchange

26.1S

J. Conroy
Journal

19X1		£	£
Jul. 28	Bills receivable	1,200	
	B. Borne		1,200
	Bill of exchange accepted by B. Borne.		
Oct. 28	B. Borne	1,200	
	Bills receivable.		1,200
	Debt of Borne re-raised on dishonour of bill of exchange.		
Oct. 28	B. Borne	10	
	Bank		10
	Noting charges on bill of exchange dishonoured by Borne.		

Ledger
B. Borne

19X1		£	19X1		£
Jul. 28	Sales	1,200	Jul. 28	Bills receivable	1,200
Oct. 28	Bills receivable	1,200			
	Bank – noting				
	charges	10			

Bills receivable

19X1		£	19X1		£
Jul. 28	B. Borne	1,200	Oct. 28	B. Borne	1,200

26.2S

B. Borne
Ledger
J. Conroy

19X1		£	19X1		£
Jul. 28	Bills payable	1,200	Jul. 28	Purchases	1,200
			Oct. 28	Bills payable	1,200
				Noting charges	10

Bills payable

19X1	£	19X1	£
Oct. 28 J. Conroy	1,200	Jul. 28 J. Conroy	1,200

Noting charges

19X1	£		
Oct. 28 J. Conroy	10		

26.3S

S. Smith
Ledger
I. Nash

19X2	£	19X2	£
Jul. 14 Sales	650	Jul. 14 Bills receivable	650
Sep. 14 Bank	650		
Bank – noting charges	10		

Bills receivable

19X2	£	19X2	£
Jul. 14 J. Nash	650	Jul. 16 Bank	635
		16 Discount on bills	15
	650		650

Discount on bills

19X2	£		
Jul. 16 Bills receivable	15		

Bank

19X2	£	19X2	£
Jul. 16 Bills receivable	635	Sep. 14 J. Nash	'650
		14 J. Nash – noting charges	10

27 Royalties

K. Dodd Treacle Mine Co.
Royalties account

Year		£	Year		£
1	Landlord	2,625	1	Operating account	2,625
2	Landlord	3,225	2	Operating account	3,225
3	Landlord	4,275	3	Operating account	4,275
4	Landlord	4,725	4	Operating account	4,725
5	Landlord	5,025	5	Operating account	5,025
6	Landlord	5,250	6	Operating account	5,250

Landlord's account

Year		£	Year		£
1	Bank	4,500	1	Royalties	2,625
				Short workings	1,875
		4,500			4,500
2	Bank	4,500	2	Royalties	3,225
				Short workings	1,275
		4,500			4,500
3	Bank	4,500	3	Royalties	4,275
				Short workings	225
		4,500			4,500
4	Bank	4,500	4	Royalties	4,725
	Short workings	225			
		4,725			4,725

5	Bank	4,500	5	Royalties	5,025
	Short workings	525			
		5,025			5,025
6	Bank	5,250	6	Royalties	5,250

Short workings account

Year		£	Year		£
1	Landlord	1,875			
2	Landlord	1,275			
3	Landlord	225			
			4	Landlord	225
			5	Landlord	525
			5	Profit and loss (short workings irrecoverable)	2,625
		3,375			3,375

27.2S

Doors Ltd
Royalties

19X2		£	19X2		£
Dec. 31	Shipton	200	Dec. 31	Manufacturing a/c	200
19X3			19X3		
Dec. 31	Shipton	400	Dec. 31	Manufacturing a/c	400
19X4			19X4		
Dec. 31	Shipton	600	Dec. 31	Manufacturing a/c	600
19X5			19X5		
Dec. 31	Shipton	500	Dec. 31	Manufacturing a/c	500

Shipton (patent owner)

19X3		£	19X2		£
Jan. 31	Bank	500	Dec. 31	Royalties	200
				Short workings	300
		500			500
19X4			19X3		
Jan. 31	Bank	500	Dec. 31	Royalties	400
				Short workings	100
		500			500

19X4			19X4		
Dec. 31	Short workings	200	Dec. 31	Royalties	600
19X5					
Jan. 31	Bank	400			
		600			600
19X5			19X5		
Dec. 31	Short workings	100	Dec. 31	Royalties	500
19X6					
Jan. 31	Bank	400			
		500			500

Short workings

		£			£
19X2					
Dec. 31	Shipton	300			
19X3					
Dec. 31	Shipton	100			
			19X4		
			Dec. 31	Shipton	200
				Profit and loss	
				(irrecoverable	
				for 19X2)	100
			19X5		
			Dec. 31	Shipton	100
		400			400

28 Departmental accounts

28.1S (a)

Expense	Basis of apportionment
Advertising	Sales
Rent and rates	Floor area
Canteen	Number of employees
Heat and light	Floor area
Insurance of stock	Average stock levels
General administration	Sales

(b)

John Dobson
Trading and Profit and Loss Account
for the year ended 30 September 19X5

	Hardware		Electrical		Total	
	£	£	£	£	£	£
Sales		59,000		29,500		88,500
Cost of goods sold						
Opening stock	2,320		2,136		4,456	
Purchases	20,000		10,000		30,000	
	22,320		12,136		34,456	
less Closing stock	2,800	19,520	2,450	9,686	5,250	29,206
Gross profit		39,480		19,814		59,294
less Expenses						
Salaries and wages	20,810		15,610		36,420	
Advertising	410		205		615	
Discounts allowed	400		200		600	
Rent and rates	1,000		500		1,500	
Canteen charges	525		350		875	
Heat and light	600		300		900	
Insurance of stock	500		440		940	
Administration	1,360		680		2,040	
Depreciation	1,800	27,405	700	18,985	2,500	46,390
		12,075		829		12,904
Commission 5%		604		41		645
Net profit		11,471		788		12,259

(c) Gross margins are approximately the same (i.e. 67%), but net margins are Hardware 19.4% and Electrical 2.6%. Expenses as a percentage of sales are Hardware 47% and Electrical 64.5%.

Electrical expenses are therefore proportionately too high. The apportionment of expenses has been carried out on a reasonably fair basis. Is the floor space allocated to Electrical too large?

Sales of Electrical department are only half sales of Hardware department. But sales staff of Electrical department are 2/3 in number and 3/4 in salaries and wages when compared with Hardware. Is staff of Electrical department too large? Can sales of Electrical department be increased without further staff costs? Salaries and wages are by far the major expense and close attention is required here.

How much of the above is due to manager of Electrical department, and how much is due to Dobson?

28.2S (a)

Allsports Ltd
Trading and Profit and Loss Account
for the year ended 30 April 19X0

	Clothing		Sports equipment		Total	
	£	£	f.	£	£	£
Sales		120,000		160,000		280,000
Cost of goods sold						
Opening stock	10,000		16,000		26,000	
Purchases (Note 1)	78,000		110,000		188,000	
	88,000		126,000		214,000	
less Closing stock	8,000	80,000	14,000	112,000	22,000	192,000
Gross profit		40,000		48,000		88,000
less Expenses						
Establishment	14,700		16,920		31,620	
Sales and ad-ministrative	7,600		6,540		14,140	
Depreciation						
Freehold property	200		200		400	
Fixtures and fittings	1,800		1,200		3,000	
Motor vehicles (Note 2)	3,500		4,900		8,400	
Staff commission	800	28,600	1,440	31,200	2,240	59,800
Net profit		11,400		16,800		28,200

(b)   *Balance Sheet as at 30 April 19X0*
Assets

	Cost	Depre-ciation	Net
	£	£	£
Fixed assets			
Freehold property	20,000	1,200	18,800
Fixtures and fittings	30,000	12,000	18,000
Motor vehicles (Note 2)	36,000	22,800	13,200
	86,000	36,000	50,000
Current assets			
Stock at cost		22,000	
Debtors		8,600	
Prepayments		300	
		30,900	
less Current liabilities			
Bank overdraft	2,300		
Creditors	5,800		
Accruals	900		
Staff commission	2,240	11,240	
Net current assets			19,660
			69,660
Financed by			
Ordinary share capital			20,000
Share premium account			2,000
Retained earnings (Note 3)			47,660
			69,660

(c) 1. To determine the profitability and contribution of each department.
   2. To compare the profitability of different departments.
   3. To assist in deciding future strategy.
   4. As an aid to internal control and audit.

Notes
1.

	£
Purchases as per trial balance	192,000
less Transfer to fixtures and fittings	4,000
	188,000

Divided between Clothing and Sports Equipment as 'balancing figure'.

2. Depreciation on motor vehicles
   Motor vehicle purchased January 19X5
   20% depreciation charged year ended 30 April 19X6
   20% depreciation charged year ended 30 April 19X7
   20% depreciation charged year ended 30 April 19X8
   20% depreciation charged year ended 30 April 19X9
   Therefore final 20% to be charged year ended 30 April 19X0.

	Cost	Depre- ciation	Net
	£	£	£
Trial balance 30 April 19X0	42,000	20,400	21,600
Depreciation 19X9/X0		8,400	
	42,000	28,800	13,200
Written off	6,000	6,000	
Balance sheet 19X0	36,000	22,800	13,200

3. Retained earnings

	£
Brought forward	19,460
Net profit for year	28,200
	47,660

29 Joint ventures

29.1S (a)

Books of Starboard
Joint venture with Port

19X9		£	19X9		£
May 4	Bank – speedboat	675	May 12	Bank – sale of speedboat	750
	Cash – repainting	40	Jun. 15	Bank – Starboard	1,000
25	Bank – repurchase of speedboat	720	30	Drawings account – boat taken over	700
Jun. 30	Bank – harbour dues	3			
	Bank – marine insurance	6			
Jul. 1	P and L – share of profit	60			
	Bank – settlement due	946			
		2,450			2,450

(b)

Port and Starboard
Memorandum joint venture account

	£		£
Expenses of Port		Income of Port	
Speedboat	730	Two speedboats	1,800
Speedboat	820	One speedboat	1,000
Speedboat	950	Boat trips	24
Reconditioned engine	120		
Insurance and harbour dues	30		
Expenses of Starboard		Income of Starboard	
Speedboat	675	Speedboat	750
Repainting	40	Speedboat for own use	700
Repurchase of speedboat	720		
Insurance and harbour dues	9		
	£		
Profit – Port	120		
Starboard	60 180		
	4,274		4,274

Workings

19X9		£	19X9		£
May 3	Bank – speedboat	730	May 31	Bank – sale of two speedboats	1,800
	Bank – speedboat	820	Jun. 15	Bank – sale of one speedboat	1,000
	Bank – speedboat	950			
	Bank – reconditioned engine	120		30 Bank – boat trips	24
Jun. 15	Bank – Starboard: receipts from one boat	1,000	Jul. 1	Bank – settlement due	946
	30 Bank – harbour dues	10			
	Bank – marine insurance	20			
Jul. 1	P and L – share of profit	120			
		3,770			3,770

Tutorial note
The above account is not required by the question, but it is a check on parts (a) and (b).

29.2S (a)   *Journal of H*

19X5	Dr. £	Cr. £
Jan. 29 J (debtor)	6,000	
Joint venture with G		6,000
Sale of goods.		
Feb. 26 Cash	6,000	
J		6,000
Cash received.		
Mar. 19 L (debtor)	2,000	
Joint venture with G		2,000
Sale of goods.		
Apr. 30 Cash	1,000	
L		1,000
Cash received.		
Apr. 30 Bad debts	1,000	
L		1,000
Bad debt written off.		
Apr. 30 Purchases	1,500	
Joint venture with G		1,500
Balance of stock taken over at agreed valuation.		

206

		Dr.	Cr.
		£	£
Apr. 30 Joint venture with G		2,700	
Profit and loss:			
Del credere commission			400
Share of profit on venture			2,300
Share of profit, etc. on joint venture.			
Apr. 30 Joint venture with G		6,800	
Cash			6,800
Cash paid to G in settlement (see workings).			

(b)   Memorandum joint venture account

	£			£
Purchases (G)	8,300	Sales (H)	6,000	
Del credere commission			2,000	8,000
H 5% of 8,000	400			
G 5% of 4,000	200	Sales (G)		4,000
Share of profit		Stock taken over by H		1,500
G	2,300			
H	2,300			
	13,500			13,500

Workings

Joint venture with G

	£		£
Profit and loss		J	6,000
Commission	400	L	2,000
Profit	2,300	Purchases	1,500
Cash – settlement with G	6,800		
	9,500		9,500

Tutorial note

A *del credere* commission is more usually met in consignment accounts. In this example it means that each party to the joint venture (i.e. G and H) will be personally responsible for bad debts on sales they have made. Therefore, although H has profits, etc., of £2,700 on the venture, the profits are offset by the £1,000 bad debt of L.

30 Sinking funds

30.1S

B.B.C.
8% debentures

19X1		£	19X1		£
Oct.	1 Debenture redemption	100,000	Sep.	29 Brought forward	100,000

Debenture sinking fund

19X1		£	19X1		£
Oct.	1 Debenture redemption (premium)	4,000	Sep.	29 Brought forward	107,208
	General reserve	100,000		30 Debenture sinking fund investments (profit on sale)	1,612
	P and L appropriation (or general reserve)	4,820			
		108,820			108,820

Debenture sinking fund investments

19X1		£	19X1		£
Sep.	29 Brought forward	107,208	Sep.	30 Cash:	
	30 Debenture sinking fund (profit on sale)	1,612		Treasury stock	35,640
				Middletown	48,000
				Electric	11,900
				Exchequer	13,280
		108,820			108,820

Debenture redemption

19X1		£	19X1		£
Oct.	1 Cash (debentures redeemed at 104)	104,000	Oct.	1 8% debentures (nominal value)	100,000
				Debenture sinking fund (premium on redemption)	4,000
		104,000			104,000

Quicksand Ltd
8% debentures (reedeemable 19X8 ie. in 20 years' time)

19X9	£	19X7	£
Dec. 31 Debenture		Jul. 1 Cash proceeds	198,000
redemption	3,200	Debenture	
19X0		discount	2,000
Jun. 30 Balance c/f	196,800		
	200,000		200,000

Sinking fund

19X8	£	19X8	£
		Jun. 30 P and L appro-	
Jun. 30 Balance c/d	4,000	priation a/c	4,000
19X9		Jul. 1 Balance b/d	4,000
Jun. 30 Balance c/d	8,210	Cash (income from	
		investments)	210
		19X9	
		Jun. 30 P and L appro-	
		priation a/c	4,000
	8,210		8,210
19X0		19X9	
Jun. 30 Transfer to		Jul. 1 Balance b/d	8,210
general reserve	3,200	Profit on sale of	
Balance c/f		investments	60
represented		Dec. 31 Debenture redemp-	
by invest-		tion (profit on	
ments	5,170	purchase)	128
Cash	4,408	19X0	
		Jun. 30 Cash (income from	
	9,578	investments)	380
		P and L appro-	
		priation a/c	4,000
	12,778		12,778

Sinking fund investments

19X8	£	19X9	£
Jul. 1 Sinking fund cash	4,000	Jun. 30 Balance c/d	4,000
	====		====
19X9		Dec. 31 Cash (sale	
Jul. 1 Balance b/d	4,000	proceeds)	3,100
Sinking fund cash	4,210	19X0	
Dec. 31 Sinking fund –		Jun. 30 Balance c/f	5,170
profit on sale	60		
	8,270		8,270
	====		====

Sinking fund cash

19X8	£	19X8	£
Jun. 30 Cash from			
company	4,000	Jun. 30 Balance c/d	4,000
	====		====
Jul. 1 Balance b/d	4,000	Jul. 1 Sinking fund	
19X9		investments	4,000
Jun. 30 Sinking fund		19X9	
(income from		Jun. 30 Balance c/d	4,210
investments)	210		
Cash from			
company	4,000		
	8,210		8,210
	====		====
Jul. 1 Balance b/d	4,210	Jul. 1 Sinking fund	
Dec. 31 Sinking fund		investments	4,210
investments (pro-		Dec. 31 Debenture	
ceeds from sale)	3,100	redemption	3,072
19X0		19X0	
Jun. 30 Sinking fund		Jun. 30 Balance c/f	
(income from		(cash available	
investments)	380	for investment)	4,408
Cash from			
company	4,000		
	11,690		11,690
	=====		=====

Debenture redemption

19X9	£	19X9	£
Dec. 31 Sinking fund cash		Dec. 31 Debentures	3,200
(£3,200 at 96)	3,072		
Sinking fund –			
profit	128		
	3,200		3,200
	====		====